KU-481-844

Kirstine Beeley

SCIENCE
IN THE EARLY YEARS

Understanding the world
through play-based learning

Published 2012 by Featherstone Education, Bloomsbury Publishing plc
50 Bedford Square, London, WC1B 3DP
www.acblack.com

ISBN 978-1-4081-554-62

Text © Kirstine Beeley 2012

Design by Lynda Murray
Photographs © Fotolia, Shutterstock
Cover photographs © Shutterstock

A CIP record for this publication is available from the British Library.
All rights reserved. No part of this publication may be reproduced in any form or by any means – graphic, electronic, or mechanical, including photocopying, recording, taping or information storage or retrieval systems – without the prior permission in writing of the publishers.

Printed in Great Britain by Latimer Trend & Company Limited

This book is produced using paper that is made from wood grown in managed, sustainable forests. It is natural, renewable and recyclable. The logging and manufacturing processes conform to the environmental regulations of the country of origin.

To see our full range of titles visit **www.acblack.com**

Acknowledgements

I would like to thank the staff and children of the following settings for their time and patience in helping to put together this book and for letting the children explore some of the ideas in it:

Treehouse Preschool, Winslow, Bucks

Prestwood Infant School, Prestwood, Bucks

MKFocus – Childminding Network, Milton Keynes

Acorn Childcare Ltd, Milton Keynes

Thanks also to Luke for continually showing me that the world can be filled with awe and wonder and to Alistair and Sarah for reassuring me continuously that my belief in what early years should be is a shared vision.

For more information on Kirstine Beeley and her training events please visit: **www.playingtolearn.co.uk**

Contents

Introduction

Imagine the scene, a small group of children huddle excitedly around a pristine new water tray, the anticipation on their faces only too obvious. The supervising adult reaches for an object from a small, uninspiring selection on a nearby table and utters those immortal words 'Will it float or will it sink?' The children offer their hypotheses and wait to see if they are correct. As the object duly sinks, it is placed on the pre-prepared chart and the process begins all over again!

Over a short time, which probably seems like an age to the children involved, the process is repeated and with each passing object the initial excitement, curiosity and enthusiasm slips away... not only from the faces of the children but from the presiding adult. Science has yet again become a chore to be endured and not a fun experience to be enjoyed.

Every time I witness this process in an early years or primary setting my heart sinks. As a former early years and primary practitioner myself (with a degree in primary science) my passion is for making science fun,

exciting and accessible to all in early years. I believe wholeheartedly that science is not just one small section of learning but is something which, when approached properly, can build solid foundations for the whole of the early years and for every child's ongoing life-long learning skills.

In my experience as an early years trainer, many practitioners sadly shy away from making science inspiring and exciting, often because of the lasting legacy of secondary school lessons full of Bunsen burners and preserved rats! In this book I want to try to demystify science and its application in early years settings. I would like to take away the veil of the unknown or the scary and show through some simple ideas and inspiring examples, how you too can put science and scientific thinking at the very heart of your play-based, child-centred, child-led approach to learning. I want to help you and the children in your care to begin to see science as something to be enjoyed not endured. I want to put the 'wow' back into science!

What is science?

Firstly, let's take a back to basics look at what we actually mean by science. We need to understand this if we are to put the acquisition of scientific skills and knowledge firmly within the realms of early learning and show that developing science learning is intertwined with modern early learning provision.

The word 'science' comes from the Latin word *scientia* meaning knowledge. The Oxford English Dictionary (Online) defines science as:

> *'the intellectual and practical activity encompassing the systematic study of the structure and behaviour of the physical and natural world through observation and experiment'.*

But this definition does nothing to break down what exactly science is within the context of children's learning or to demystify it as a subject. It just helps to make science sound more scary and difficult to understand than it actually is! So here I will have a go at explaining it myself.

Making sense of the world

Science is all about exploring and understanding the world around us. It is a subject which has developed in parallel with human evolution as a way of making sense of the world. From the dawn of human civilisation one of the things which sets us apart from other mammals and animals is our instinctive curiosity, a need to know what, how and why things work. From this in-built 'need to know' stems science.

For many of us our first experience of science as a subject begins at secondary school with the focus on Biology, Chemistry and Physics which all stem from a need to make sense of the world around us. Biology, the science of all things living; Chemistry, the science of what things are made of and Physics, the science of why things work the way they do. They are not so scary when viewed through a more simplistic eye I hope?

So, with curiosity and exploration at the heart of human nature it makes sense that science begins not in school but from the moment we are born. From the second we arrive in this world, and actually even before this, we start to use all five of our senses to make sense of the world around us. We start to develop our scientific skills and understanding. We begin to do what scientists all over the world have done for centuries. We try something, learn from the experience, think of a question and use our senses to find an answer to that question. In early development those questions could be 'What will this taste like?' or 'What will happen when I mix this porridge with this sand?' but the process is the same as a scientist in his expensive university laboratory asking, 'What will happen if I collide this molecule with this one?' It just means that the small child can try things and find out (experiment) on a much shorter timeline and with a slightly smaller budget! Both are 'doing science'. Both are trying to make sense of the world around them.

However, science as a subject has many traits which are unique and which need to be understood if you are to provide good provision in your setting.

Knowing it all

Many practitioners I meet and talk to express a kind of fear of science. They are worried about not knowing the answer to a child's question or scared of not knowing why or how something they want to share with the children happens. But worry not! That's what science is all about — **you don't need to know all the answers!** No-one does because science is just what we know about the world at that point in time and through scientific investigation and exploration the 'what we know' of science is constantly evolving and changing.

For example, in Galileo's time you would have happily accepted as scientific fact that the world was flat. Technology and scientific knowledge has moved forward and enabled us to view the world differently and we are now able to see the true shape of the world. A great example of how quickly science can change comes when you look at Pluto. Many people, myself included, went happily through our school years being informed and accepting that Pluto was a planet. In 2006 scientists reclassified it and in 2012 it is no longer viewed as a planet due to a number of factors including its size and the way that it behaves in its orbit of the Sun (although there is now discussion about whether to reclassify it again... a case of watch this space).

This recent scientific development has ongoing repercussions for educational establishments across the world. How many still have library bookshelves full of titles including Pluto in their definitive planet list? And this recent scientific development has yet to filter through to all primary teachers, some of whom are still teaching the old theory.

So next time you worry about not knowing the answer to a child's question, just remember science by its very nature is about making the most of the knowledge you have and trying to find out the answers to the questions you don't know the answers to. A simple 'I'm not sure... let's see if we can find out' is a great way to embrace all that science is about and to encourage children to do the same.

The language of science

> 'We are sometimes in danger of forgetting how challenging it can be for children to express themselves, especially in relation to ideas and experiences that are new to them.'
>
> Feasey (2000)

Science may well be intertwined with the very fabric of our children's learning but that doesn't mean to say that it hasn't got some very unique qualities. Science has, for instance, its own language which we, the practitioners, are the key to unlocking in our children.

It is not enough to provide children with lots of opportunities for exploration and investigation as part of their ongoing play. We cannot just give them science-based experiences and expect them to have the correct terms to hand. We, the adults, need to offer our children the language of science, almost as a gift. It's simply another way of helping them to make sense of their ever-changing world.

Children playing happily in a water tray may well find that some things go to the bottom of the water while others stay on top, but making the connection between this process and the correct terminology, that is, float and sink, needs our input. However, be warned! This imparting of such linguistic knowledge can lead to the whole essence of early science discovery and exploration being squeezed out in favour of mundane, language-based activities (see the original description of a floating and sinking activity in the Introduction to this book!).

Adult intervention needs to be enthusiastic, relevant and most of all a part of the child's ongoing play experience. A helpful 'When things go to the bottom, we call that sinking' as part of ongoing water play serves much better than a monotonous sorting of individual items into plastic float or sink circles. 'We're going on a metal hunt' (armed with magnets of course!) as a follow-on from the ever-popular 'We're going on a bear hunt' is so much more engaging than sitting down to sort objects into metal, wood and plastic!

So what kind of language do we need to offer our children? Science language tends to fall roughly into three main categories:

1. The language of enquiry

2. The language of objects and equipment

3. The language of processes

The language of enquiry

Here you are encouraging language based around exploring and investigating. It is the language of 'What if…', 'How…', 'If…' and 'Why…'? It is giving the children the language tools to be able to ask questions of the world around them and to begin to formulate theories to be tested and situations to be investigated.

The language of objects and equipment

This aspect of science language is easier for adults to get to grips with as it is concrete and tangible. You can hold, show, touch, feel, smell and explore many objects and pieces of equipment which children can use in their explorations. By talking with children as part of these investigations it is easy to see opportunities for building this type of language. Carefully-labelled drawers and investigations areas (see Chapter 3) will help to build science language in many other areas of play across your setting.

The language of processes

This is where you help children to build the vocabulary that they need to explain what they find out, using terminology such as melting, sinking, moving, loud and so on. Again, this should be introduced sensitively, as part of children's ongoing play, to offer an additional tool to help them make sense of the world around them.

We, as early years practitioners, must plan for and be aware of opportunities to help children experience and develop their use of science language across all three categories.

Unique skills to get the job done

In an environment of child-led, child-initiated and child-focused learning, we adults have an essential and key role. Giving children the opportunity and means to explore, question and investigate the world around them involves using many objects and pieces of equipment. Some are everyday items such as sieves, jugs and trowels while others are definitely 'science specific', such as magnifying glasses, magnets and water play syringes. All need adult input when it comes to the correct way to use them.

One little boy I know spent weeks happily playing in the water tray spraying all and sundry with a large plastic syringe until one day I observed him filling it by completely removing the inner pump part of the syringe. A quick demonstration by me on how to pull the end up underwater and the whole process of water play took on a renewed enthusiasm. His new skill of quick refill resulted in a very wet and soggy me!

It is our role as adults to ensure that we identify opportunities to introduce science-specific equipment that could potentially enhance children's existing play and ensure we impart the best way to use this equipment safely. We are the key to helping children build the skills they need to explore science within the guidelines of good health and safety. Once children have gained these skills they are better set to build on their personal investigations and explorations through their play. Making the equipment accessible on an ongoing basis (Chapter 3) will result in them being confident, inquisitive explorers.

Developing science-specific attitudes

If we are to put the 'wow' back into science in early years (and primary) settings we need to nurture positive attitudes towards science both in the children and the adults involved. We need to develop a 'can do' attitude by everyone to enable children to access their science learning as part of good, child-led opportunities.

To allow science exploration to be child-centred and child-led we need to be nurturing a positive sense of being able 'to do' in our children. When they are drawn to ask 'Why?', 'What if?' and 'How can...?' they need to know that as a setting and as a staff team you will help them to answer their questions. They need to know that you will answer with a 'I don't know …let's see if we can find out' or 'Let's try it shall we?' not 'Let's see what we can find out in our next science session or after we've had P.E … or storytime'.

As Piaget noted all those years ago:

> 'Children are not empty vessels to be filled with knowledge. They are active builders of knowledge — little scientists who construct their own theories of the world.'
>
> Cited in Singer and Revenson (1996).

The embracing of child-centred science approaches can falter in some primary schools where there may be pressure from scheduled times for the use of shared areas such as the hall, computer room or garden. However, if practitioners are to embrace the child-led nature of learning, then they have to have a 'can do' attitude to taking forward children's questions and ideas. Practitioners need to acknowledge the benefits to both learning potential and positive self-esteem of taking what a child asks and helping them to answer their own questions. Remember, if a child's questions and ideas are constantly met with delays or a lack of enthusiasm they will eventually stop asking!

A good positive attitude to science from all practitioners will directly impact on a good positive attitude to science and exploration in our children. Everyone in your setting needs to be encouraged to want to know about the world around them.

Chapter 2

Science and the EYFS

For the purposes of this book I am focusing upon the English Early Years Foundation Stage framework (EYFS) but the child-centred nature of the discussions and their impact on approaches fits equally comfortably within the Welsh Early Years Foundation Phase, the Scottish Early Years framework and the Northern Ireland Foundation Stage framework.

Traditionally, within the EYFS framework much of the specific reference to science has come within the Learning and Development elements. However the positive provision for supporting emerging scientific skills, language, knowledge and attitudes is also at the core of the other main areas of focus within EYFS provision. Science is very much at the heart of A Unique Child, Positive Relationships and Positive Environments as well as Learning and Development.
I want to take a brief look at what some of the documentation says and to place it firmly within the jargon-free real world of working with small children!

Science and the proposed 2012 EYFS framework

Knowledge and Understanding of the World, newly renamed Understanding the World, is not one of the three prime areas of focus of the proposed EYFS framework (these are: Emotional Development, Physical Development and Communication and Language). However, this chapter will highlight how science exploration as part of good, everyday play-based experiences can contribute to all areas of the EYFS and help children to build the skills for life-long learning not only in early years, but in primary school and beyond.

Understanding the World

Children should be guided...

> 'to make sense of their physical world and their community through opportunities to explore, observe and find out about people, places, technology and the environment'.
>
> DFE (2011)

I have already talked about how 'making sense of the world' is actually exactly what science is. The key part of this requirement is about supporting children to enable this to happen. Focus should be on the 'can do' attitude that we have already identified as being at the centre of delivering our child-led approach to finding out about the world. It is worth remembering that this is about the children making sense of their world not us telling them how we see our world!

> 'Children know about similarities and differences in relation to places, objects, materials and living things. They can talk about the features of their own immediate environment and how environments might vary from one another.'
>
> DFE (2011)

Put quite simply... this is about children learning through good quality play-based exploration and allowing them the opportunities to build the skills to do this safely.

Experiment or experimenting... that is the question?

> 'They can make observations of animals and plants and explain why some things occur, and talk about changes, including in simple experiments.'
>
> DFE (2011)

This seems a good place to ask this question as we can now see how it directly fits within the proposed EYFS framework. However, your personal concept of what we mean by an 'experiment' can potentially have a huge impact upon how you deliver science in your setting.

Many of us are left with a lasting legacy of secondary school science 'experiments' which followed a tried, tested, traditional and completely ingrained format. Ask a room full of early years practitioners to recall what is included in an 'experiment' and they will reel off the following:

- **Questions** (hypothesis)

- **Equipment** (what we need to use)

- **Method** (what we did)

- **Results** (what we found out)

- **Conclusion** (did we find out what we thought we would?).

Although this content is technically correct in its defining of an 'experiment' it might be more helpful, in early years particularly, to view experiments as an overall process with many different elements. Our focus on it as a complete and all-encompassing process can potentially impact upon how we plan for and deliver science-based learning. Practitioners can get caught up in a perceived need to include all of the above elements within any and every science-based activity when in actual fact, it may be better and more appropriate to just focus on one element of experimenting. In other words, it's better to focus on one specific skill than to try to force all of the elements into one activity. For example, it might be that your identified and planned focus for a

day, a week, or even a half term is on the children's ability to ask questions. As a result all activities and opportunities that you offer will be geared towards encouraging this skill. Another science focus might be the children's ability to choose and access the correct science equipment and use it safely to help them answer their own questions.

When viewed in this way, the process of assessment, evaluation and recording of science in the early years begins to focus more on the processes of science investigation than on having to have a chart or a table or something else as an end product of an 'experiment'. This then allows you to be more creative with what and how you record science learning (see Chapter 7).

It is really important to remember the significance of 'process rather than product' if science is to benefit children's life-long learning skills. Science offers the opportunity to focus on key skills such as questioning, trying out theories, investigating and adjusting our thinking. These skills can be used throughout the children's learning in all other areas and subjects. By focusing in on the processes of science rather than the end product we are giving children much, much more than just science knowledge and understanding.

The significance of science in other areas of EYFS delivery

A Unique Child

> 'Every child is a unique child, who begins learning at birth and can become resilient, capable, confident and self-assured.'
>
> DfE (2011)

> 'Children learn better by doing, and by doing things with other people who are more competent, rather than just being told.'
>
> DFES (2007)

It is imperative that we value children's individual view of their world and support them in their play to explore and investigate their own questions and theories. By doing this, not only will individual children build knowledge but they will feel valued and supported as unique human beings with a unique view of the world. By providing 'creative' approaches and putting some 'wow' into science we are more likely to engage children in the process of learning (see later chapters for ideas about how to get creative with your approach to science).

Something to reflect upon

When a child has been playing in the water tray all day and has discovered that all of the blue things sink, is it our place to say 'No, not all blue things sink' or, through careful planning and reflection, do we offer extra opportunities for that child to revisit their view? This might include offering some situations which ask the child to challenge and build on their existing knowledge. It may be that you provide some blue objects that float and some differently-coloured objects that sink as part of the ongoing water play.

Positive Relationships

'When working with young children, the exchange between adults and children should be fluid, moving interchangeably between activities initiated by children and adult responses helps build the child's learning and understanding.'

DFE (2011)

'Children learn to be strong and independent through positive relationships with their parents and carers and with others, including their key person at their early years setting. '

DFE (2011)

Being able to observe our children and know when to intervene to build on and support their learning is crucial in helping them to move forward. The more children know you are there to help and support them in their approach to exploring their world, the more confident in themselves and their own abilities they will become.

Remember: A can-do approach by adults supports a can-do approach in children.

Positive Environments

'A positive environment in which children's experiences are planned to reflect their needs, and help build their confidence, and in which there is a strong partnership between early years practitioners, parents and other professionals – is crucial if children are to fulfil their potential and learn and develop well.'

DFE (2011)

'A rich and varied environment supports children's learning and development. It gives them the confidence to explore and learn in secure and safe yet challenging indoor and outdoor spaces.'

DFES (2007)

If children are to grow into confident independent science explorers who are happy to 'have a go' at investigating the world around them, it is imperative that we set up our environment to support this ethos. The next chapter concentrates on what you the practitioner can do to create an environment which doesn't just enable scientific learning to happen but which positively encourages it as part of everything you do.

Chapter 3

Enabling your early science environment

This chapter is very much about the 'who', 'what' and 'where' of science provision in early years. Planning for good early science provision is not just about having a positive approach as a practitioner but also requires a reflective look at how you set up your physical learning environment to encourage child-led exploration and investigation. Developing and enabling an exploration and investigation-led environment is about looking at and auditing the types and amounts of equipment you have on offer as well as considering a number of other factors, including accessibility and types of provision. You need to ask yourself questions such as:

- What kind of exploration do we offer?

- Do we vary the levels of adult intervention?

- Is there scope for a wider range of situations to be available?

- Does the accessibility to resources impact upon the child-led nature of investigations?

- Do we have enough resources available to allow children full access to a wide range of scientific learning all of the time?

- Do we have the kinds of resources that stimulate children's imagination and investigative thinking?

- Is there provision for scientific exploration both indoors and outdoors?

Types of science exploration

As early years practitioners we are aware of a need to provide a balance of both adult-led and child-initiated opportunities. Although there is much debate about the ratio of this balance, with many leading practitioners calling for an ideal 80 per cent child-initiated to 20 per cent adult-led, I feel that within the context of this book it is much better and more useful to look at what we actually mean by adult-led and child-initiated activities and discussing their relevance to early science exploration and its delivery.

There are many ways of visually representing the interrelationship between the differing types of interaction. The diagram below shows that, even within those activities, where the process is a shared experience there are differing levels of adult input,

making some activities more adult-led than others. It may be easier to look at a particular theme and then examine the different ways we can deliver learning approaches within that theme.

The example I have taken is that of growing seeds, a common activity in many early years settings throughout the spring term in the UK, when the growing season is in full swing. So how can the varying levels of adult/child interaction be applied to this popular theme? For the purposes of this discussion I have chosen to group shared learning into a single category. It is, however, worth remembering that the level of adult input can vary and although a shared activity, it may turn out to be predominantly child-led.

| Adult-led | Shared learning (bias towards adult-led) | Shared learning (bias towards child-led) | Child-initiated learning |

Adult-led: demonstrating how to plant a seed

Adult-led activities are planned with the intention of the adult passing on or 'teaching' very specific skills and facts that the children can then go on to use in their own child-initiated learning. Here, the adult would show the children how to use all of the relevant equipment (pots, compost, trowels, seeds and so on) to successfully plant a seed.

The emphasis is on the passing on of skills and knowledge, not on the process. The adult should be looking for opportunities to use and point out specific language such as 'plant', 'dig', 'grow' and 'seeds'. The activity may lead to children planting seeds as they copy and develop their planting skills, although this is not the planned objective of this type of activity. The product of such a session, the planted seeds, may then be used as a stimulus for future discussion and exploration as part of other planned activities later on.

Shared learning: exploring seeds together

For this activity the role of the adult is to work alongside the children, making ongoing observations of their discussions and learning. The adult should offer a potential route for exploration through well-thought-out, open-ended questions which the children may or may not decide to follow through on.

During this activity the adult and children together are offered lots of different types of seeds (sunflower, poppy, sweetcorn kernels, flower seeds, beans, conkers, acorns, pumpkin seeds and so on). The idea is for everyone to explore the selection and for any discussions to lead the direction of potential investigations. The adult would be looking for opportunities to respond to children's comments with open-ended questions which give children the starting point they may need to take an idea forward.

After listening to and joining in with a discussion about the differing size of the seeds, the adult may offer a question such as 'I wonder if a big seed would grow into something big' or 'Do you think that the smaller seeds make smaller flowers?' The open-ended nature of these questions is almost challenging children to respond. It is stimulating their enthusiasm and leaving them wanting to find the answer. However, the direction that any subsequent investigation might take will be more child-led and the adult will have to then take on a supporting role, helping the children to take their exploration forward.

This 'light the blue touch paper and stand well back' approach is not always easy for some adults who have a clear idea about where they feel the exploration should go. It takes careful planning, time and practice to be able to offer an open-ended question, facilitate the children's responses and then observe the outcomes. In this situation the children may decide to plant a variety of different seeds into one pot or many; they may choose to plant only small or large seeds; they may choose to search for small or large seeds on plants to see where they come from. The direction is driven by the children, *not* the adult.

Child-initiated learning: exploring seeds and stuff!

For this approach to work, the practitioner will need to think of the potential for exploration within the scope of the theme and provide as wide a range as possible of equipment and resources for the children to explore.

This activity would probably start in much the same way as the shared activity, with the provision of a range of seeds for children to investigate but with the addition of lots of other equipment to potentially enhance their thinking and learning. The resources provided might include:

- **pots** (lots of different sizes and made from lots of different materials — clay, terracotta, metal, plastic and so on)

- **planting materials** (compost, soil, leaf mould, mud, clay, flour and sand)

- **garden tools** (watering cans – big and small, trowels, hand forks, spoons, sieves, dibbers – sticks for making holes for seeds to go in, and so on)

- **containers for planting** (dependent upon the amount of space available these can range from a couple of old tyres lined with plastic and filled with compost, to wooden planters made from recycled wooden pallets or just a load of big plastic planter pots)

- **seed trays and gravel trays** (gravel trays are bigger than seed trays and make great small-world trays when not being used for seed planting!)

Ideally, you want to offer opportunities for children to be able to dig and plant individually, in pairs and small groups. Remember some children will choose to plant seeds according to accepted

gardening practice and will want their seeds protected while they are nurtured, while others will go through the process of sowing, watering, weeding and harvesting all within half an hour.

The point of this activity is to provide lots of opportunities for children to take their exploration of seeds in whichever direction they feel they want to. The adult acts as facilitator, there to offer help and resources when requested and to ensure safe practice prevails. They also take the opportunity to observe the children's interactions, assess learning and develop ideas for future activities to build on their observations of this activity.

Please let the children guide us through their world, instead of us forcing our world on them. Only then will we be privileged enough to witness the wonder that an autumn leaf can offer or the full potential of a muddy puddle on a rainy day.

Points to consider

It is worth pointing out that the timing of these activities has the potential to vary according to the type of interaction that is planned. The shared and child-led parts of this planned theme may traditionally be offered during the spring, mainly because the adult-led part is best suited to spring planting. However, autumn offers an opportunity for children to observe at first hand the seeds in their natural environment and to begin to make sense of where seeds come from (not just out of a packet at your local DIY shop or garden centre!). Alternatively, an exploration of seeds in winter can lead to lots of exploration around birds and small animals and their winter feeding habits.

We should observe the natural world around us (as we ask the children to do) and let what we see inspire us to offer learning opportunities, not just stick to a rolling plan or themed provision just because that's how we've always done it.

So to recap, we should be looking at the potential for science planning and making sure that we offer a good balance of adult-led, shared and child-initiated opportunities for exploration and investigation.

Resources and equipment

A multi-million pound industry in the UK exists to provide classroom equipment and resources. As practitioners we are often tempted by the pages of glossy catalogues to spend our limited cash on resources aimed at specific areas of learning and development. Science is a strange one when it comes to resourcing. Yes, there are resources which are very 'science specific', equipment that children would not generally come into contact with outside of science exploration. Magnets, magnifiers and bug-catchers all fall into this category and we do need supplies of these essential resources if we are to teach the children the skills to use them safely within their own explorations.

However, much of what is marketed as 'science equipment' is easily sourced elsewhere and quite often much more cheaply. Ask yourself, do you really need to spend in excess of £100 on a purpose built dark den? Or could the money be better spent on providing lots of more open-ended resources which encourage curiosity and exploration (and if you buy a few cheap black or dark blue sheets from your local supermarket you have your dark den as well!).

When looking at what equipment you need to support early science it's worth going back to our definition of what science is – a way of making sense of the world around us through purposeful play. With this in mind, much of the equipment you will be looking at exists to enhance existing play-based learning across all areas (see Chapter 4).

With this view in mind much of the equipment you will be sourcing can either be purchased cheaply from everyday shops and supermarkets or can be sourced from parents and grandparents who are often keen to play a useful part in their child/grandchild's ongoing learning (see Chapter 9).

Rather than offer up a recipe-type definitive list of all the things you should be looking to have available I have chosen to integrate suggestions for resources into some of the activites later in the book. The idea is that in this way resources can be viewed within the context of the learning which they can support. You can then make informed decisions about how to supplement your existing resources.

What you do need to keep in mind when selecting resources, is whether they support children in their own exploration. Are they open-ended enough? Can they be used in numerous different situations? Will they help children find the answers to their own questions about the world?

That said, once you have selected and sourced a wide range of equipment to help children become emergent scientists you have to look very closely at how you make these resources accessible to them. There is no point in spending hundreds of pounds on equipment if it goes into a cupboard only to be brought out by the adult either as part of an adult-led activity or when it fits with a planned theme at the same time every year. You need to look at ways of making science resources available every day as part of the children's ongoing play-based learning.

Investigation stations — indoors

One of the best ways of making resources available every day and also giving practitioners a very visual focus for science-based investigation is to have an 'investigation station'. This is an area where all of the basic 'science' equipment is freely accessible to children at all times and which also provides lots of points of interest aimed at sparking excitement and curiosity. For decades, practitioners have been happy to include a 'nature table' in their settings, displaying seasonal natural objects for children to look at, pick up and explore. An investigation station takes this idea and runs with it!

A wide range of objects and equipment can be displayed (not just natural resources), with the common denominator being that everything is there because it aims to spark interest, curiosity, discussion, questioning and excitement in the children. The station can combine this focus for interest with storage of additional science equipment so that children can extend their exploration of the objects in the area or dip into the resources to further explore their learning in other areas of the setting.

NB: Remember that, as with other areas throughout the setting, interest diminishes over time and the objects displayed in your investigation station need to be refreshed on a regular basis.

Suggested equipment/resources to have in your investigation station:

- **magnifying glasses and pots with magnifying lids**

- **magnets** – different sizes, shapes and strengths

- **torches** – different types (battery operated, rechargeable, pump action and wind up dynamo, solar powered)

- **coloured filters, coloured sweet wrappers** (from well-known chocolate selection tins!), **and kaleidoscopes**

- **mirrors and shiny objects** (spoons, tin foil, foil papers, etc)

- **pipettes, droppers and plastic syringes of different sizes**

- **natural object selections** (include conkers, acorns, pine cones, seeds, bark, stones, pebbles, crystals, feathers etc).

- **seashore selection** – shells (big and small), driftwood, starfish, seahorse, dried seaweed

- **binoculars** – include several pairs (available cheaply in spring from pound and camping shops)

- **fabrics, textiles and other materials** – include sheep's wool (washed and dried), sand paper, silk, fur fabric, hessian, jute, voile, cotton etc

- **animal bones** (boiled, washed, and prepared properly animal skulls are a great talking point for small children)

- **timers** – sand timer (different sizes and times), gloop timer, oil clock, wind-up cooking timer, digital stopwatches

- **tape measures** (big and small) and **rulers**

- **collecting pots** – clear pots and petri dishes for children to collect and store their finds

- **cameras and voice recorders** – to record their findings as they go.

Investigation stations – outdoors

I have always liked the idea of a 'nature table' reflecting a wide range of natural objects for exploration and investigation. However, I do feel it is better suited, whenever possible, to being outdoors. This puts the objects within their natural environment and helps children to enhance their understanding of the natural world while actually working within it.

Investigation stations can just as easily be set up outside, with cheap sturdy plastic storage box units used to house the selection of investigation materials. These can then, if needed, be wheeled back in at the end of the day along with the bikes and trikes.

If you have the space, then making a permanent investigation station from natural materials (a low level plank of wood on some tree stumps works brilliantly) helps to enhance your outdoor provision. It provides a focal point for displaying children's natural finds as well as some other natural talking points. Where better to look closely at a birds' nest, some moss covered bark or a wormery?

As with all resources in early years, make sure that all drawers and boxes containing resources are clearly labelled with both pictures and text to allow children easy self-selection and to help them in returning resources when they have finished.

Discovery bottles

Discovery bottles are a great addition to any investigation station, indoors or out. They use small clear plastic drinks bottles to offer a secure container for many different materials, textures, scents and so on which children can explore freely. Discovery bottles do exactly what they say on the packet, they encourage children to explore and discover, to pick up, to look, to shake and to share.

Use clear plastic drinks' bottles in a variety of shapes and sizes. Make sure they are the type with screw-on tops (not pull-up spouts – except for smelly bottle – see page 21). Wash and dry the bottles thoroughly and then add your contents. Place some strong glue (hot glue guns are ideal) inside the rim of the lid and screw back on, ensuring that when the glue dries the contents of the bottle are safely sealed within the bottle preventing any potential choking hazard from small parts or safety issues with liquid contents. For added safety, put coloured tape around the bottle neck and top to secure it further and to add extra colourful interest.

Suggestions for contents

Many different types of discovery bottles are possible — you are limited only by your imagination. The internet offers lots of ideas as does *The Little Book of Discovery Bottles* by Ann Roberts (Featherstone). When making up your bottle collection try to make sure you have bottles which encourage exploration using as many senses as possible (they don't particularly lend themselves to exploring the sense of taste – for hopefully obvious reasons!).

Some of my favourites are as follows:

Liquid mixers – half fill the bottle with baby oil. Mix some water and food colouring in a jug and then add to the bottle so that it is nearly full. Seal and tilt the bottle to see a colourful wave motion as the oil and water refuse to mix. If you shake the bottle vigorously, you will see small amounts of the oil mix throughout the water and then if left, it will slowly separate again as you watch. This is a very calming lava lamp type effect. Why not make a few in different colours or add some glitter to the mixture for extra effect?

Magnetic mysteries – place a selection of metal and non-metal objects into your bottle. Half of the challenge for this one is finding a range of small enough objects to go through the neck of the bottle — try paperclips, split pins, marbles, coins, hairgrips, action figures and so on. Make sure you include some metal objects which are coated so that they don't look obviously metallic, for example, a plastic-coated paper clip. Now seal the bottle and use a large bar magnet or magnet wand to explore the objects inside the bottle. If leaving out for children to explore then attach the magnet wand to the neck of the bottle with a short piece of string.

Floating feathers – place a selection of different-coloured and sized feathers into a bottle. Allow the children to shake and explore the bottle. They will enjoy watching the different colours as the feathers fall slowly down through the bottle.

Sounds abound – fill a selection of bottles with materials which, when shaken, make different noises. Dry pasta, rainbow rice, lentils and jingle bells are all great.

Access to additional equipment

I am a realist, and, having worked in many early years settings I know only too well the impact of storage issues on facilitating child-led learning. It is not always possible to have all of the equipment you would like permanently available to children at all times. However, there will be equipment that you own which, with a little imagination, can be made accessible.

Why not try photographing larger pieces of equipment such as camouflage nets and bubble makers and displaying them on a board with Velcro so children can bring you a picture of anything they would like to have out in their play? Make enhancement baskets or boxes for common themes such as 'Windy weather', 'Rainy days', 'Water exploring' and 'Minibeasts'. Photograph the sets so the children can indicate if they would like those sets of equipment out as well as the investigation station. This method allows children to self-select resources while alleviating some of the pressure to have everything out all of the time.

Smell familiar – place some food essence onto some cotton wool and place into the bottle (use plastic drink bottles with pull-up spouts). Glue the twist part of the lid on so that the contents cannot be accessed. Now pull up the spout and squeeze the bottle and as you do this sniff the contents. Use essences such as orange, strawberry, vanilla, lemon, almond and so on. You can also use herbs such as basil, mint, lemon balm, curry plant and lavender or add a few cloves or star anise for some more unusual smells.
NB: Never use essential oils as these can cause serious allergic reactions.

Look what I found – fill a large plastic fizzy drink bottle (2 ltr) with small coloured beads (shop around as cheap versions can be found). Alternatively use rainbow coloured rice. Collect a selection of small objects of interest – small plastic bugs and characters, a penny, a marble and so on. Photocopy or scan the objects and laminate the sheet. Then place the objects into the bottle, seal the top and shake. Now use the picture sheet as a reference and see if you can find all of the objects inside.

Sparkly shakers – fill a bottle with glycerin (available from pharmacies). Add a selection of sequins and sparkles as well as a couple of coloured marbles. Seal the top and shake. The glycerin is clear but very thick and the sparkles travel really slowly through it. Marbles move slowly down through the liquid.

A finding-out board

As well as an investigation station and access to wider resources, you need somewhere that focuses attention on what you are trying to find out. A 'finding-out board' is a great way to celebrate children's curiosity and develop confidence in asking questions for enquiry. In the absence of a suitable available display board, a piece of coloured mounting board covered in plastic film can be fixed at child height for easy access and ongoing revisiting.

The idea is that as children come up with questions about their world, the questions are then written (by adults or children) on speech or thought bubble-shaped cards (you can buy speech bubble-shaped sticky notes which work really well too). These are then placed on to the 'What we want to find out ...' board and used as a reference point for ongoing discussion and planning. The board allows a focal point for practitioners when looking at what child-led interests will guide their future planning and act as a point for reflection when talking to children.

The boards are great for boosting children's self-confidence, as they know that their questions will be noted and acted upon. They will also enjoy going back over the questions and recapping on what they managed to find the answers to. This method also makes some allowance for school settings where timetabling of assemblies, hall time and so on may mean it is not always convenient to follow a child's questioning through immediately. By adding their question to the board, you are acknowledging the need to find out at the earliest opportunity. Make sure you don't end up coming back to the questions after too long a time frame when the children will have lost interest and enthusiasm (and possibly faith in you!).

As well as making sure that you have specific resources available for science investigation and exploration, it is important that you also look at the potential for science enquiry as part of your integrated provision in other areas throughout the setting. The next chapter aims to look at common areas of continuous provision and suggest some ways to enhance play in these areas to encourage scientific enquiry as well as looking at the kinds of science learning which take place as a result of different types of play.

Chapter 4 Science around your setting

Although this book is about 'science' and looks at how science differs from other subjects, it is also very much about how science exploration and investigation is rooted in all that we do in early years. Other books focus on the primary national curriculum and look in depth at 'experiments' to look specifically at, for example, materials or forces. In early years (and in an ideal world also in Key Stage 1) we should be looking at how science skills and knowledge can be accessed through creative play across the setting.

It is, therefore, more important to look here at some of the areas of continuous provision which will already be in your setting and to highlight how these areas support science learning. Early years provision is very much about seeing the learning potential of one creative, child-centred activity across a number of areas. As one of my colleagues once put it, 'It's about seeing what's right in front of our eyes and realising that there's so much learning already going on'. It is also about providing children with the opportunity to revisit their thinking and build, develop or change their existing knowledge and beliefs by offering them lots of opportunities to explore the same area of learning in hundreds of different ways.

Within each of these areas you need to be looking for opportunities for children to 'do science', to be looking at what things are made of, what happens to things as they play, to ask questions, to try things out and to use their senses to explore the world around them and begin to make sense of it all.

Water play

The virtues of water play have already been explored earlier when I discussed how not to do floating and sinking! Exposing children to many and varied opportunities to play with water will, with support, give them ample opportunity to explore the idea of floating and sinking within the context of their play. Water play offers all the opportunities that sand does; to pour and play with, to explore how it behaves in various situations. Like sand, it can be altered in many ways to enhance the children's knowledge and allow them to revisit their thinking many times.

Water play experiences need to be offered both indoors and outdoors and on many different scales, from small individual mixing bowls to large paddling pools and water trays. (Please remember that safety should always be carefully considered.)

Some of the things you can do to enhance children's water play exploration are discussed here but many more will stem from the children's own discussions, so please try not to have palpitations when the children decide they want to add water to the digging area, sand to the water or if teddy from the role-play corner goes for an impromptu bath! Stay calm and see the learning potential… water makes mud change its consistency and properties allowing it to be poured, sieved and splashed in. Sand sinks in water and can be sieved or poured and wouldn't it be great to see how many bubbles teddy wants in his bath or how long it takes for him to dry out! The potential is always there, we just have to open our eyes and begin to acknowledge it.

Things to do to enhance scientific exploration through water play:

1. **Change what's in the water** – add various things to the water over time to stimulate discussion and exploration as the children play (be mindful of skin allergies). Add washing-up liquid, soap, shower gel, bubble mixture, baby oil to coloured water (to see it divide and separate), vegetable oil to puddles (to see the rainbows), cellulose paste (without fungicide), toothpaste, shaving foam, bicarbonate of soda, salt (add enough so that things which used to sink will now float), sparkles and glitter, dried cereals including rice crispies and porridge (and watch them as they change state).

2. **Change the colour of the water** – add food colourings and paints (food colouring makes for transparent water including black). Paint produces a more opaque water where objects can be hidden at the bottom of a deep green or blue sea!

3. **Change the temperature of the water** – vary from cold (including ice cubes) to warm. Combine with colours to prompt extra exploration and discussion (some children automatically assume that blue water will be colder than red water – offer them opportunities to challenge this thinking by supplying cold red water and warm blue water).

4. **Change the smell of the water** – as with sand (page 26) you can add lots of different scents with food essences being particularly good – try peppermint or strawberry as well as vanilla, lavender and rose petals.

5. **Change the tools you provide** – give children lots of different tools with which to potentially explore their water source, be it indoors or out. A paddling pool or a puddle will enhance and provide great opportunities for exploring science language, understanding and skills.

Equipment to have available includes:

- **wide selection of containers** – different sizes, shapes and materials, clear and opaque, with and without tops

- **funnels** – large and small

- **scoops and spoons** – various sizes and materials (good for children to experience that metal spoons become cold in cold water and warm in warm water). *NB: Never allow children to touch a metal object that has been left outside in freezing conditions as cold can burn their skin.*

- **straws** – different colours, lengths (you can get 1 metre long straws from party shops) and shapes (curly and straight)

- **plastic tubing** – different sizes and lengths

- **plastic guttering and pipes** – in different lengths

- **whisks** – different sizes, made from different materials and working in different ways (hand whisks and wind-up whisks)

- **droppers, syringes and pipettes** – droppers and pipettes are worth investing in cheaply from educational suppliers (see resource list on page 19) as are plastic needleless syringes which can be purchased in lots of different sizes. Add turkey basters for added large-scale exploration.

- **pouring items on different scales** – includes saucepans, washing-up liquid bottles and camping kettles as well as full-sized watering cans – not everything has to be child-sized in life!

- **a wide selection of materials that float and sink** – not just your standard rock and rubber duck! Try to make your selection interesting, exciting and creative. Include objects which challenge thinking like large objects that float (such as large wax candles) or small objects that sink (small dense plastic toys often sink). Include rocks that float (pumice) and hollow objects which when they fill with water will cause the object to sink slowly. Keep changing what is available regularly to continually build on and challenge children's thinking.

The list is endless and the golden rule is that if the children find it interesting and want to explore it in the water and if it is safe to do so – then let them! Oh and remember… rainy days offer great opportunities for exploring water!

Something to try – floating and sinking fruit

Fruit is familiar to most children and always provokes lots of excitement and discussion. Most children and many adults relate floating to size or weight, but it actually depends upon an item's density. Playing with a wide variety of fruits and vegetables in the water tray can help to revisit existing understanding and also challenge thinking.

Large heavier fruits such as a coconut may float while smaller (but more dense) fruits such as pears may sink (remember this if anyone challenges you to pear bobbing!). Try floating a satsuma or an orange and then peel and try again, is there any difference? (Sometimes taking the skin off makes the fruit more dense and more likely to sink or partially sink.)

Sand play

Much of what early science experiences are about is exploring different materials and discovering what we can do with them and how they change when we play with them or add them to other things. The tactile nature of sand allows children lots of opportunities to work with it, to hold it, pour it, sieve it and mix it with other things while making full use of their senses. Much can be done to enhance sand play to give more opportunities for exploration over time including adding:

- colours – add food colouring and then leave to dry out.

- scents – add food essences like lemon, orange or strawberry or dried herbs such as lavender, curry plant leaves or lemon balm.

- textures – add other things like rainbow rice, sawdust, or dried pasta or cereal – children have great fun sieving sand if there's something to sieve out of it! Try adding water and some cheap jewels (an old necklace unstrung can work but small gem stones are easily available cheaply online), give the children sieves and let them go panning for jewels? Or have a go at making sand mousse – a frothy tactile sand mixture or your own version of moon sand (see recipes).

All of these experiences build on children's understanding of how sand and other materials behave as well as encouraging them to use their senses to explore. Even just trying to get the right mix of sand and water to get a sandcastle to come out of a bucket and stay standing is utilising lots of science-based skills and understanding about what things are made of and how they behave.

Sand mousse

You will need:

- play sand (in a tray)

- bottle of washing-up liquid

- warm water

What to do:

Add some washing-up liquid and warm water to play sand and mix until you have a frothy mousse texture. The amounts will vary dependent upon the amount of sand you use. Add colours or glitter for extra effect but the strange texture of the sand alone is often enough to inspire children's play for ages.

Moon sand

You will need:

- 6 cups play sand

- 3 cups cornflour

- warm water (about a cup full)

- food colouring (optional)

What to do:

Mix the cornflour and the water together to make a smooth paste. Then gradually add the play sand until you have a soft (not sticky) mixture. This is now ready to play with. Seal in an airtight container when you have finished. If you reuse the sand, it will need reviving with a few tablespoons of water.

Add food colouring to the initial cornflour mixture to make coloured sand.

NB: this product only has a limited shelf life due to the water which has potential to become stagnant.

Messy play

The purist science teachers of primary schools across the country would happily have children 'experiment' with sorting, matching and testing materials as well as using forces to bend, twist and stretch things. Yet messy play provides it all, in a much more exciting, fun and engaging child-friendly way, so much so that it amazes me that more primary teachers don't adopt it in their classrooms! After all, you can twist, pull and flatten play dough; you can squish, squash and squeeze clean mud and slime (see recipes) and you can stretch, roll and mould cooked, coloured spaghetti. Imagine what can be done with shaving foam, gloop, rainbow rice, tin foil, tinsel and shark-infested custard!

Messy play offers an ideal opportunity for children to freely explore the properties of materials (whether it squashes, pours, twists or makes great patterns!) and to revisit their thinking over time as other messy play activities are offered. Each time children revisit they are using their senses to explore, question and make sense of the world and to learn more and more about what things are made of and how they behave.

This is so much more exciting that twisting a rubber band, bending a paperclip or pulling a piece of sticky tack (all of which I have seen in primary schools). Messy play offers children the chance to make sense of materials as part of their integrated play experiences.

Slime

This is a variation on Gloop, which offers a much stickier consistency.

You will need:

- 1 packet of cornflour

- 1 bar of moisturising soap grated (or boxed soap flakes)

- warm water

- food colouring, paint and glitter for added extra effect

What to do: Add warm water a little at a time to the cornflour until you have a stiff mixture which behaves like a solid when you hit it and then a liquid as you hold it in your fingers. Now add the grated soap and mix to make slime (you may need to add a little more water).

Add food colouring or a bit of poster paint to turn your slime into purple alien slime or a green crocodile swamp.

Clean mud

This recipe gives you a sticky material which behaves and feels like mud but which is white and clean! It is great for small-world play with polar animals.

You will need:

- soapflakes or grated soap (one with a moisturiser is best for this)

- white toilet tissue

- warm water

What to do: Add the soap flakes to your container or play tray. Tear up the toilet tissue into small pieces and then add warm water and mix together. Add more until you have enough mixture at the correct sticky consistency.

NB: Be aware of potential skin allergies – use hypoallergenic soaps if this is an issue.

Creative play

As with messy play, creative play offers an array of opportunities for children to play with, explore and investigate what things are made of and how they work. Creative play when it is child-led and not about children copying a 'Blue Peter' type 'Here's one I did earlier' product, gives children the chance to get messy and try and retry their hand at using different materials and tools. It allows them to visit and revisit their thinking about different materials. Humble paint can offer lots of opportunities to explore using senses when you add different things to it or try painting with things other than paint.

Ideas for widening the opportunities for exploration and investigation:

1 **Texture your paint** – add different materials to make the paint behave differently. Include things such as sawdust, sand, cornflour, tapioca and washing-up liquid. Add icing sugar and the paint will dry shiny, add salt and it will dry crystalised. Try puffy paints that puff up in the microwave (see recipe on page 59). The thicker you make the paint, the more the children will need the chance to explore it with tools other than a paint brush so remember to offer plastic knives, wooden sticks or even to encourage children to use their fingers and toes to explore.

2 **Scent your paint** – you can add lots of things to paint to make it (and any resulting pictures) smell great. Why not try food essences such as lemon, orange, almond or vanilla (smells like chocolate!) or add chopped up herbs such as star anise (smells like liquorice), cloves, lemon balm, curry plant, mint, basil, or lavender? Adding these to paint really encourages children to explore their sense of smell as part of their play and beats sniffing yoghurt pots!

3 **Painting without paint** – use other materials to paint and mark-make to help children explore properties of materials in a fun creative play situation. Try painting with mud, clay, coloured milk (if you paint on to toast you can toast it and eat!) or even with melted chocolate. Try using coloured chalks dipped in a puddle to paint outdoors or coloured water to paint on to kitchen roll. All of these ideas allow children to use their existing painting skills and build on them while discovering what happens to chalk in water or chocolate when it melts or cools.

NB: Never use hot melted chocolate with children for safety reasons. Wait for it to cool and add in some chocolate ice-cream sauce or vegetable oil if you want it to stay runny.

As well as paint play experiences, children will build on their knowledge and understanding of what things are made of when they use items to make other creations, for example, junk modelling boxes, glue, wood, string, elastic bands, ribbons and glue. It is this constant open availability of a wide range of materials for children to play with that makes early years such a great place for science exploration to take place. Children's thinking is being challenged and built upon at every twist and turn.

And let's not forget the possibilities for investigation, exploration and excitement that musical creativity can offer. Allowing children ample opportunity to interact with and explore the sounds that lots of instruments make not only builds their awareness of sounds and develops their sense of hearing but also builds on their existing knowledge of what things are made of. Exploring the sounds that you can make using different spoons and sticks on a saucepan drum set as it hangs from the garden fence builds on your understanding about metal, wood and plastic while you get to have lots of fun and make lots of wonderful music!

Please don't let your children be turned away from the science of sound by sitting them around a table and asking them to make almost identical yoghurt pot shakers (not only is this not creative but it's incredibly boring and helps children learn little about the properties of materials or sounds). Why not try a more open-ended approach or link it to a story to make it relevant and interesting? (See The Happy Hedgehog Band ideas on page 52).

Role play

This is another area where lots of science is probably already happening but just not being acknowledged as science. Role play provides a fantastic opportunity to make the children see that science can be and is exciting and amazing.

Children are already exploring materials and properties as they make mud pies outside in their café, as they play with their umbrellas in the puddles and as they follow dinosaur footprints in the mud. There are also opportunities to add extras to children's role play which can specifically encourage scientific play. Try having a 'potions-mixing' laboratory complete with pouring funnels, flasks and droppers. Add bicarbonate of soda, coloured white vinegar and lemon juice, cola and ice cubes and watch the look on the children's faces as they mix and create. (Bicarbonate of soda and vinegar or lemon juice will fizz and froth as will cola when ice cubes or salt are added.) Try combining this with a story like *What's in the Witch's Kitchen?* by Nick Sharratt (Candlewick Press) for added excitement and enjoyment (see Chapter 8).

Adding some oversized men's white shirts (with the sleeves rolled up) and scientists' plastic safety goggles (available from some pound shops in the DIY section) gives the children the chance to play at being scientists. It leads to some amazing language and imaginative play. Of course, make sure you have lots of 'science specific' equipment like binoculars and magnifiers available freely for children to integrate into their own play scenarios.

Making science an exciting part of play helps children to see at an early age that it can be fun and enjoyable. This is really important, considering that a recent survey showed that young children are becoming less and less enthusiastic about science by the time they get to Year 6 (Ruddock et al 2004).

Small-world play

As with larger scale role play, there is lots of science already occurring in much of the small-world play you offer. Children working with plastic, wood and metal resources will be building on their knowledge of these materials. Playing with trains, tractors, cars and trucks gives ample opportunity to explore how things move and what happens when we push or pull things in our setting.

When you combine elements of outdoor play or messy play with small-world play the scope for exploring and investigating expands still further. Why not make green gloop (cornflour and water) and help the children to create a dinosaur swamp? How about purple slime (see recipe on page 27) and add aliens for an extra-terrestrial play experience? Shaving foam or clean mud (see page 27) make excellent bases for polar or snowy explorations, as does a tray of ice cubes or real snow. Try artificial snow (available online in powder form) or ice cubes on a hot sunny day.

Adding small-world figures to coloured puddles and mud patches allows the children to explore materials in a natural environment and you can introduce natural materials such as using moss, bark, leaves, twigs and shells to make a fairy wonderland. A gravel tray filled with water-logged moss makes a great crocodile swamp! The possibilities are limited only by the children's imagination but with a little bit of thought and some careful observation you will soon be able to see the science that is happening as a natural part of the imaginative play.

Block play

There is a great opportunity here, not only to explore materials (as you should be providing your children with blocks made from many different materials in many different sizes) but to explore physical forces at first-hand. Building towers, bridges, castles and roads gives the children an excellent chance to observe first-hand the work of gravity. Providing different-sized blocks gives the children a hands-on way of exploring heavy, light and 'really heavy'. The different shapes allow the children to experiment with rolling, stacking, leaning and falling. They can also explore their influence on the movement of objects.

Include large blocks, logs and log slices as well as smaller bricks, tree blocks and plastic sets. All will offer the children different experiences and the chance to try and retry their ideas on different scales and using different materials.

Books and information

Science has its own language and children need lots of opportunities to explore this through science-based books as well as through talk during play. Science-based information books about tractors, space and baking bread all give children the chance to share texts which interest them as well as building continually on their existing knowledge. Make sure your book stock includes lots of science-based fiction and information books.

If you are going to have books to support your investigation station then rather than have them standing up on the display (where they often can't be reached by the children without them accidentally demolishing everything within a metre radius), fill a small basket with relevant books. Put this either on the floor or nearby at accessible height so children can easily flick through and self-select books that they want to look at and share.

Chapter 5

Science and outdoor play

'The best classroom and the richest cupboard are roofed only by the sky.'
Margaret McMillan 1914

The importance of outdoor play in children's ongoing early development is now widely acknowledged, with outdoor learning having equal value to indoor learning. Instead of just including it as another area of provision within the previous chapter, I have deliberately decided to consider it separately for a number of reasons. Not only to give it the level of importance it deserves within overall early years planning, but also to emphasise the unique opportunities offered by outdoor environments across all areas of early learning, including science.

The play areas described in the previous chapter can all be offered outdoors as well as in; but the outdoor environment can also offer unique experiences to further enhance existing science skills and knowledge.

Here I would like to consider what makes the outdoors so unique and offer some ideas for enhancing science learning outdoors as part of ongoing purposeful play provision. When reading and considering these ideas, it is important to bear in mind that all aspects of outdoor play should be planned for alongside your planning for indoor play, not just as an add-on to your planning for messy, creative or small-world play.

Economies of scale

The outdoor environment offers children the opportunity to explore situations, activities and materials which, due to their size and scale, could not physically be accommodated easily indoors. They can throw paint around on huge sheets of paper; hurl spaghetti spiderwebs; push and pull large bikes, trikes, tyres and logs; work together with a large parachute on a windy day or build an igloo from snow bricks on a winter's afternoon. The sheer space offers the children the chance to run, jump, shout and scream without the constraints of walls and ceilings. They can explore their own body movements and experiment with sounds in a way that only the outdoors can offer.

Interactions with nature

Outdoors offers the children a brilliant opportunity to experience at first-hand all that nature has to offer and to explore and observe living plants and creatures. Even the smallest of outdoor spaces can share an array of plant life and birds and with a little planning and creativity it is easy to coax minibeasts and other wildlife into your outdoor environment. Too many children do not have the chance to explore the natural world and some people believe that children are in danger of becoming 'nature phobic'. We really must embrace all the opportunities we can to allow children to be curious about, to look at and explore, to touch and feel, to ask questions and to talk about as many natural situations as we can.

The ever-changing seasons and weather

With the ever-changing seasons comes the ever-changing weather. Nowhere is this more so than in the UK where we can often experience many different kinds of weather within one season or even within one week or a day! The outdoor learning environment offers children the opportunity to experience all of these changes first-hand. They can physically experience the wetness of a puddle or the cold of snow, see ice melting or feel wind blowing on their faces. At every twist and turn, there are amazing chances for children to use their senses to build on their knowledge and to observe the impact of the weather on their immediate environment and the materials within.

To ensure that children have the richest and most varied opportunities to build their science learning (and all other areas too!), we must embrace all of these differences, offering exciting activities which grab children's imaginations and run with them!

Again, as with the previous chapter, there is much that can be done to enhance the opportunities for scientific learning and these can only be touched upon briefly here. Reflecting upon your own ongoing practice and continually observing the children's interests and learning will provide you with many more ideas. However, here are some suggestions to get you going.

The wonderful world of nature

'When children are outside they cannot help but learn about the world around them, with the changing weather and seasons under their noses.'

Leicestershire Early Years Team www.leics. gov.uk/outdoor_learning_publication-2.pdf

There is much that we can do, even in the smallest of outdoor areas, to encourage wildlife and to develop opportunities for children to experience it first-hand through play and exploration. Even if you have no grass at all, it is still possible to make the area nature rich. Use cheap or recycled planters or tyres to grow flowers, herbs and vegetables. Grow small trees, bamboo plants and large grasses in pots. The latter make a lovely sound as they blow in the wind. All it takes is a little imagination and a commitment to the potential of outdoor learning.

Sensory gardening – developing a sensory garden with your children allows them to interact directly with nature as well as stimulating their senses outdoors.

- **Grow a wide range of aromatic plants** such as lavender, lemon balm, lemon thyme, curry plant, mint (you can get all sorts of mint including pineapple and apple mint), fennel, chocolate cosmos (yes, the flowers do actually smell of chocolate!), rosemary and basil. Encourage the children to care for the plants as well as being able to touch, sniff and explore their scents.

- **Look for ways to add sound to your garden** – wind chimes can be purchased in a wide variety of different materials (metal ones sound so different from bamboo ones). Alternatively, make some by tying together bamboo cane pieces and adding strings of jingle bells to blow in the wind. Make a musical wall using old pots and pans and utensils strung up and add lots of different materials such as wooden sticks and metal and plastic spoons to be used as beaters.

- **Find creative ways of stimulating the children's sense of sight** – make mobiles from natural materials such as feathers, fir cones and conkers strung on sticks. Try reflective ones made from old recycled CDs strung with beads and ribbons. String wicker balls, found in bags of pot pouri, with ribbons and hang where any breeze can catch them. Add Perspex mirrors to old brick or shed walls (try to get concave as well as convex – the ones that curve both ways!). Metal spoons strung up will catch the light. Dream catchers made from twigs tied together and interwoven with string, feathers and leaves will make even the dullest of corners look stimulating.

Growing a wildlife garden

From small bugs, butterflies and insects to birds and small animals there is much that you can be doing to provide sources of both food and shelter for your local wildlife. You will need to look at what plants you use and the kinds of wildlife these will attract. For instance, buddleia bushes are great for attracting butterflies but it is worth remembering that caterpillars will only eat their preferred food sources, so, for example, cabbages will feed the caterpillars of the cabbage white butterfly.

The following websites all contain lots of helpful hints on how to get started with your wildlife garden:

- www.sussexwildlifetrust.org.uk/wildlife/index.htm

- www.bbc.co.uk/gardening

- www.mywildlifegarden.co.uk/index.html

- www.warwickshire-wildlife-trust.org.uk — they have a great downloadable booklet with lots of ideas

- www.naturalengland.org.uk — a lovely range of colourful downloadable leaflets on how to encourage minibeasts, birds and mammals into your garden

- www.direct.gov.uk/en/ Environmentandgreenerliving/ Greenerhomeandgarden/Greenergarden/ DG_064418

Remember that a well-planned wildlife garden should offer support for wildlife in all seasons.

- **Try to find ways to add texture to your garden** – make textured tiles from carpet, sandpaper and so on, as well as making your own by pushing objects into clay squares before drying. Attach these to a wall to encourage children to explore with their hands (you can even make big ones and sink them into the path as stepping stones).

I am not ignoring the fifth sense of taste and obviously many of your herbs and vegetables grown in your outdoor space can be tasted but I would recommend this being done under adult supervision.

NB: Ensure that the children are not encouraged to pick or eat anything without a grown-up with them.

Making the most of the weather

'Weather has to be "worked with" in order for children not to miss out.'

Harriman (2006)

In the UK the weather is ever changing and continually offers us chances to interact with it. There seems to me to be two key factors in utilising the weather's full potential in early years generally, but particularly in science learning. First and foremost is attitude. Having the right kind of attitude to outdoors is vital. We need to be providing children with the opportunity to go outdoors, whatever the weather. There is a well-known phrase in Scandinavian countries: 'There's no such thing as bad weather, only bad clothing!' Try to overcome any fear of the cold and the wet and acknowledge the learning potential offered by outdoor all-weather play.

The second element to success in early outdoor science learning would have to be preparation. Not in the sense of planning activities to within an inch of your life but having sets of resources available to allow children to make the most of the changeable elements at the shortest of notice.

One of the best ways I have seen of being as prepared as you possibly can (after all, when working with children, you can never be prepared for all eventualities!) is to develop some weather boxes, bags or baskets. The storage is a matter of choice and should be based upon what works best for your setting. For some, having clear plastic boxes is ideal, for others hanging drawstring bags on fences may be a better, less permanent solution (make sure strings are short enough not to pose a safety issue) and baskets may offer a good, removable resource bank for settings who have to pack away every day. The choice is yours and may be adapted once you have reflected upon what works best for your children (don't be afraid to adapt and change your mind!).

The idea of weather boxes (I'll use this term for convenience) is to bring together a selection of objects and items which can be accessed when you are experiencing a particular kind of weather and which will encourage the children to explore the potential of such conditions further still. These are in addition to any boxes you may already have to ensure children have the appropriate clothing and sun protection for the weather conditions. On the following pages are some suggestions of what you may like to include in your weather boxes but the potential is limited only by your imagination. More things can always be added as children discover new uses for everyday items.

Windy day box

- **handheld windmills** (shop bought and handmade)

- **ribbon streamers** (lengths of ribbon tied to wooden spoons and wooden curtain rings so the children can run around with them)

- **washing line and pegs** – for pegging out clothes, materials, anything really and watching them blow in the wind

- **flags** (big and small) made from lots of different materials including paper and fabric

- **parachute** or large sheet to experience the wind as a small group

- **feathers** – throw into the air and see the wind blow them

- **light fabric scarves** (or pieces of chopped-up voile curtain) that the children can run around with and trail behind them in the wind

- **streamers** (paper as well as ribbon)

- **bubble mixture and bubble wands** – bigger multi-bubble wands are great in windy weather!

- **a silver survival foil blanket** – great for running around with in the wind

- **children's umbrella** – so they can really feel the strength of the wind

- **frisbee.**

Sunny day box

- **sunglasses** with different-coloured filters *(NB: Make sure that children know never to look directly at the sun)*

- **pieces of coloured cellophane** (chocolate and sweet wrappers are good and cheap!)

- **perspex mirrors** – so children can explore reflections

- **shiny objects** like spoons, tin foil, costume jewellery that will catch the light *(NB: Make sure you check metal objects on sunny days in case they become too hot to touch)*

- **chalks** – so children can draw around shadows to see them move and change

- **old CDs on strings** – great for catching and reflecting the light

- **perspex prisms**

- **sun cream** – you can never have enough sun cream and children can explore using it in their role play, on dolls or could even use it for messy play which will help to get over the dislike of applying it that some children have *(NB: check for allergies).*

Icy day box

- **salt** – table and rock so the children can explore the effects of it on ice and frosty surfaces (always be mindful of safety in icy conditions)

- **DIY paint brushes** in different sizes – so children can paint on frosty surfaces with warm water

- **magnifying glasses** – so children can explore close up the beautiful patterns made by ice and frost

- **perspex mirrors** – so children can see their warm breath

Foggy day box

- **torches** – lots of different sorts (battery operated, dynamo and solar powered). Why won't they work on a foggy day?

- **glow sticks** – you can get in lots of different shapes and sizes (keep the spent ones as children often think they carry on glowing forever and enjoy trying to find out which ones work and which ones don't)

- **reflective objects** – find cheap reflective items in pound shops for safety use on bicycles and cars such as a safety triangle, reflective high visibility jacket, reflective arm bands and bag tags

- **fluorescent items** – include things which are just fluorescent colours like paper etc. and see if you can see them in the fog

- **lights** – camping lights and bike lights are good and can include battery and wind up versions as well as flashing ones. You can even buy lights that come with a built-in glow stick!

- **mirrors** – can you see in the mirrors in the fog?

- **flashing, light-up toys**

- **sound Instruments** – including horns and things you can blow.

This box basically has most of the equipment in it that you may have for a dark den exploration but allows children the opportunity of exploring the contents in a completely different scenario.

Rainy day box

- **containers** – various sizes, shapes and materials to catch rain in and to hear different sounds as rain falls

- **chalks** – to chalk around puddles and see them get bigger and smaller

- **food colouring** – to add to puddles to change colours

- **powder paint** – for mixing into puddles for puddle painting

- **bubble mixture** and washing-up liquid to make puddles bubbly

- **vegetable or baby oil** – added to puddles gives a rainbow effect

- **marbling inks and paper** – for marbling pictures from puddles

- **sponges**

- **funnels**

- **waterwheels** – from sand/water play toys

- **shower curtain** – children can sit under it and hear the rain or drape it over a table or climbing frame to make a den that is noisy and which they can see the rain through

- **umbrellas**

- **watering cans.**

Enhancing seasonal outdoor play

With the seasons come many different play opportunities and it is important that we embrace these as they occur. Your weather boxes can be used at any time of the year when the weather dictates. In 2011 in the UK, we saw hot sunny days, torrential rain, gale force winds, fog, frost and snow all in the month of October!

Here are some suggestions for activities you may like to try in your setting at various times of the year (although challenging children's ongoing thinking is always key so why not try some of them in opposite seasons?).

Spring

- **Bubbly puddles** – add washing-up liquid to puddles and let children whisk them up with metal whisks and wooden spoons to create bubbly puddles which will reflect light in the sun. How can you make more bubbles? Bigger bubbles?

- **Giant bubble** – make up some strong bubble mixture and pour into a builders' tray or a paddling pool. Place a small hoola hoop into the mixture. Carefully help a child to stand in the middle of the hoop and then gently lift the hoop up. With a little trial and error, you can get the right mix to get a big bubble that will go up the full height of the child, effectively letting them stand inside a giant bubble!

- **Puddle painting** – this can be done in a number of ways depending on the materials available. Add food colouring to puddles and the children will just enjoy mixing the colours together. Mix powder paints into puddles with a range of brushes (including toothbrushes and loo brushes — unused!) In both cases, once mixed, you can lay paper on to the puddle to lift off a watery puddle print. Marbling inks can be used in the same way and give some really dramatic effects.

- **Puddle sizes** – use coloured chalks to draw around puddles and then watch as they get bigger if it rains or smaller as the sun comes out. Exploring what happens to coloured chalks in puddles is also a great activity.

- **Building a nest** – spring is the season of nest building in trees and hedgerows across the land. Children can observe birds collecting sticks and twigs and can help them by hanging out net bags (the ones oranges and satsumas come in) stuffed with soft nest-building materials such as sheep's wool, feathers and dog hair. Allow the children to build their own nest. I don't mean a tidy little bird-sized one as I've observed many a time in creative areas, but a full child-sized nest! Give children access to lots of sticks, twigs, leaves, grass, feathers and so on and let them build to their hearts' content. Not only will there be lots of investigation of materials going on but also lots of talking and excited storytelling.

Summer

- **Giant ice cubes** – take a selection of different-shaped and sized plastic or foil containers and add different-coloured water. Add in a range of objects including leaves, flowers toys, plastic coins, plastic gems, buttons and so on and freeze. Empty into a play tray or potting tray and let the children explore and watch as the ice melts to reveal its treasure over time. If you part-fill a pot with one colour of water and freeze, you can then add other colours and refreeze to create rainbow ice. Try Alistair Bryce Clegg's idea and freeze natural objects to make numbers in ice for added mathematical discussion, see **http://abcdoes.typepad.com/abc-does-a-blog/2011/05/ice-ice-baby.html**

- **Shadow play** – allow the children to explore shadows using shadow puppets and sticks in bright sunlight (why this activity is always done inside with torches is beyond me!). Place a stick in the ground and mark the shadow with chalk. Leave it for a while and revisit to see if the shadow has changed or moved.

- **Snow and ice in summer** – exploring snow and ice in summer gives the children the opportunity to observe melting at first hand. Add a bag of ice cubes to a tray and let the children play. (Pour salt on to the pile and the ice will melt and refreeze almost instantly making the ice cubes stick together in an ice mountain. Add coloured warm water to the top of your ice mountain and watch as the colours work their way down through the ice.) Fill a tray with artificial snow (available cheaply online and from pound shops at Christmas) and let the children enjoy polar ice cap play. The artificial snow also feels cold to the touch as you add water to it and mix due to a chemical reaction.

- **Ladybird house** – cut bamboo canes into short lengths and fill an old plastic milk bottle with the side cut out. Alternatively, roll up some cheap bamboo lawn edging. Hang up your ladybird house in a nearby tree or hedge to offer a safe place for ladybirds to live (and to take shelter over winter eventually). Ladybirds are great for your garden as they feed off aphids and other small creatures which can do a lot of damage to your plants.

- **Tree faces** – collect natural materials such as moss, leaves, twigs, flowers and so on. Take a ball of clay and mould it on to a tree trunk to make a face. Add the natural materials to make hair, ears and so on. Leave the clay to harden in the sun. This is a great way to explore the changing nature of clay and natural materials, enhance your outdoor area and give lots of starting points for imaginative play and talk.

Autumn

- **Painting with mud and clay** – mix up different-coloured natural paints using mud, clay, and other materials (crushed chalk makes a lovely white paste and powdered red brick mixed with water makes a great red colour). Now make brushes using sticks, leaves, grass and string and allow children to paint.

- **Autumn mobiles** – use all sorts of natural materials collected from out and about, include conkers, wood, moss, leaves, feathers and fir cones. Add string and wire to make beautiful hanging nature mobiles to enhance trees and outdoor areas. Ribbons and jingle bells can be threaded on for extra effect.

- **Nature collages** – use natural objects like acorns, fir cones, feathers, twigs, leaves, moss, shells, pebbles and so on. Let the children make their own large-scale natural collages on the ground. Allowing children access to a wide range of natural materials all year round means this is a great one for any season!

- **Parachute and seed play** – take a small parachute or a small sheet and get the children to stand around the outside. When the parachute is tight, add acorns, conkers and feathers to the centre and work together to move the autumn objects around. Which ones move the easiest, the fastest and so on? How high can you get them to go? Which ones roll? This is great fun, especially when accompanied with singing of popular songs and rhymes.

Useful resources

- For more seasonal outdoor activity ideas and free downloadable resources visit: **www.woodlandtrust.org.uk**

- For lots of exciting ideas to use in your setting visit **www.abcdoes.com**

- **Effective Practice in Outdoor Learning** by Terry Gould (Featherstone) is packed full of inspiring and practical ideas for outdoor experiences.

Winter

- **Ice painting** – brush warm watered-down paint on to icy or snowy surfaces in winter to make lovely outdoor paintings. In snow, fill washing-up liquid bottles with warm coloured watery paint and squirt on to white snowy surfaces.

- **Ice cube painting** – freeze poster paints in ice-cube trays, then use the frozen paint cubes to make patterns and paint on to paper or directly on to the floor outside. (This is a great idea for repeating in warm sunny weather too!)

- **Ice light catchers** – fill a foil food tray with water, lay a length of string into the water with a loop left outside. Add a selection of natural objects that you find including leaves, twigs, flowers, pebbles and so on. Leave outdoors overnight to freeze. In the morning, remove  from the container and hang somewhere where the light can catch it. (This is another good one for doing in spring or summer when children can observe the ice melting, but obviously it would have to be frozen in the freezer!)

- **Bird seed pictures** – use different-coloured seeds and grains to make a picture on the snow or a frosty lawn. Take a picture to record your creation and then leave the seed for the birds to eat.

- **Igloo ice bricks** – if you get lots of snow then make snow bricks by pushing snow into square ice-cream containers and build a snow wall or an igloo.

I hope you can see that the outdoor learning environment is key to providing lots of exciting and unique opportunities for children to develop, explore and revisit their scientific thinking and skills. Make sure that you plan equally for outdoor and indoor activities and learning. And don't forget your outdoor investigation station!

Chapter 6

Science questioning

Once you have reflected upon, reassessed and enabled your environment to support ongoing exploration, encourage inquisitiveness and foster curiosity, it is worth having a look at how you facilitate children's scientific investigation skills. In previous chapters, we have discussed the role of the adult in instigating enquiry. This chapter looks at the role you play in children's ongoing exploration and how best to offer open-ended situations which encourage children to find their own solutions.

Open-endedness is a concept that applies not only to the kind of resources that you provide but to the play scenarios you offer and the kinds of questions you ask. For children to be able to truly follow their own individual learning journey, we have to be offering them this approach.

Yet open-endedness is a concept that practitioners can sometimes struggle with. If we have an idea of something we think would be fun for the children to make, it's sometimes difficult not to guide them towards a set end product. If we want to explore a certain concept, it's sometimes hard not to steer the discussion away from its natural child-led course and keep to our own planned agenda. Asking questions for which there is no right or wrong answer can be hard if we want to check that the children know the answers about particular areas. Yet for good science to take place (and early learning in general), it is an approach that we really do have to get to grips with.

The adult's role in scaffolding learning

The key to offering an open-ended approach at the same time as supporting children's ongoing learning is knowing when and how to intervene and when not to. We need to learn to listen and then offer input at a point when it is most needed rather than to steamroller over children's play and learning with our own agendas. One of the hardest things is to be able to step back and let children get on with their own play while observing their learning and looking for times where a need or an opportunity offers itself and we can then step in. Remember, science is about the children making sense of their world, not us telling them about ours!

Once you have mastered the ability to step away from play and actually observe learning taking place, you need to be mindful of the potential for ongoing learning. Constantly ask yourself can I see where this play might be going? Is there something I could offer at some point which might enhance the play further? Would asking another open-ended question spark enthusiasm and another line of enquiry? Can I add resources that might challenge the thinking that I am observing?

Within early learning, your role as the adult is to make sure you know what learning should look like.

By that I mean both know your learning theory, but also get to grips with and familiarise yourself with the learning requirements of the EYFS framework. Learn to use them not as a tool for box-ticking at the end of a set period to check whether a child has learned something, but as a tool for supporting ongoing learning.

If you know what the next step to learning should be, then you are more likely to be able to offer play situations which can enhance children's thinking and be working towards the next step in their learning. If you are knowledgeable about the ways children learn, you are more likely to be able to offer play opportunities which support and develop every child in your care. Even with science you should still be looking for ways to offer learning in different styles: visually, audibly and kinaesthetically (science you can see, hear and get physically involved in).

So, you've mastered the art of observing, you've managed to identify the learning which is taking place, you know what the next step for their learning is and you have an idea of something you can ask to take the learning forward. We now need to take some time to look at questioning and how we can ask questions to get the best responses from our children.

Questions for answering — not for the sake of it

As practitioners we are sometimes guilty of just asking children questions because we want to check what we think they know. We ask questions which we already know the answers to because we want to tick a box to say they have achieved that standard or they know that concept. But will the children's response in such a situation really give us the answers we want? Will it really give us an understanding of their learning? How often when you ask a child a question like, 'Will this float?' or 'What makes a flower grow?' do we get a real insight into their knowledge and understanding?

This is key to early learning because it's not just about knowing a fact, it's about the child's ability to revisit that knowledge and apply it in a wide variety of situations. It's about the child playing in water trays, puddles, paddling pools and bowls and learning through exploration and discussion with adults and peers that things may float not only in one situation but in many situations.

It's not about just giving you a straight 'yes' or 'no' answer to a question. This is an answer which quite frankly might be an indicator of knowledge but may also be a guess (be mindful of a child searching your face for a flicker of recognition) or a copy of what they heard their best friend say five minutes before (remember children are always out to please!).

So try to move away from asking questions you already know the answer to and begin to show children that questions lead to finding out answers. By mastering the art of open-ended questioning, you will be offering situations where children are free to find their own answers by their own means and you, the practitioner, get the privileged position of being witness to all of the learning that can unfold in front of you as a result. Offer questions which challenge children to explore, to investigate and to find out. By careful observation and recording of the play learning you see you will be able to tick those boxes without having to ask questions for the sake of questions.

What kinds of questions?

In general the rule in the English language is that an open-ended question is one which does not have a closed answer (a right or wrong answer). If it can be answered yes or no, the thinking would usually be that it is not open-ended as there is no room for additional discussion. However, within the context of early science, some questions which may traditionally be viewed as closed questions, can lead to surprisingly opened solutions and investigations. This is because they offer up a 'science challenge'.

They challenge children to find out the answer and although children may need support initially to be confident enough to follow their own lines of enquiry as a result, they can eventually be very creative in their solutions. Challenging questions are those which tend to ask children 'Can...', 'How...' and 'Could...'. 'Can you build a bridge?' 'How can we make soup?' 'Could we make a new mixture for the wizard?' These challenging questions, offered within the context of the children's play and experience (making them relevant to the children) can excite and enthuse the discovery and inquisitiveness that is at the heart of science learning.

When developing open-ended challenging questions in science, the rule seems to be that the shorter the question the more potential it has for open-endedness. The difference, for example, between 'Can you find out what's inside this fruit?' and 'What's inside?'.

The thing about challenging questions is that to make sense and to offer potential for investigation, they have to be asked within the context of the children's play, within the scope of their own understanding. On page 53 I look more closely at some of the opened-ended questions you could be offering children to get them started on a scientific line of enquiry which is rooted firmly within familiar stories.

> 'Science learning in early years is about curiosity and wanting to know how and why… It is about being so fascinated by something that you want to touch it and watch it and tell everyone about it.'
>
> Keogh and Naylor cited in De Boo (2000)

It is worth noting that as children get more used to exploring as a result of challenging questions, they begin to ask their own questions more confidently. This is something we need to be aware of. We should not just be looking at developing our own questioning skills but those of the children in our care, constantly looking for ways to show them that we value their questions and encouraging them to ask more.

Person-centred questions

It is not only the types of questions that we ask which will influence the quality of children's responses but also the way in which we ask them. It is worth remembering that done in the right way, person-centred questions can offer a means of individuals expressing their views without feeling there is a right or wrong answer. It is the difference between asking a child 'What happened to this plant?... you tell me (child's name)' and 'What do you think might have happened to this plant?' However, for this to work it has to be asked in a tone of voice and within an overall ethos which lets children confidently know that their opinion will be valued and does not necessarily have to be the same opinion as the person next to them.

This is an ethos which values all opinions as equal and welcomes different views. Keep the Pluto situation (see page 6) at the back of your mind always! Science is forever changing and none of us have all the right answers.

Recording learning or hoarding?

If ever there was a subject which stirs up debate and emotion, and which highlights the influence of a traditionally 'top-down' education system, it is the recording of information in early years. Some practitioners will argue that they must have a written recording of anything that moves in their setting and the reason given is so often 'because the teachers in the next class or in the school want it'.

In my opinion, this view is one which needs to be challenged within the context of a play-based, child-centred early years framework which has been put in place for all children up to the age of five (so in theory also including some children for part of Year 1 in England!). We perhaps need to look at what and why we record information and consider ways of providing this to our colleagues further up the system in a way that is useful but which does not detract from what early years learning should be about. There are many ways of recording what or how a child has learned something without having to get them to put pen to paper, let alone do it once or twice a week in a book (as I have been witness to in some reception classes).

Why do we record?

Let's start with why we record in early years. This is a question that you as a staff team should be asking yourselves regularly and constantly re-evaluating your answers. In early years, recording is about having a record of a significant point in a child's learning development which shows you that they have acquired new knowledge, made sense of an existing skill or concept or shown a need for reinforcement. The reason for recording is to inform us so that we are able to help the children to develop further. Recording is therefore for the children not for the adults.

I am a realist and I understand that some education settings can be highly emotionally-charged places where views differ greatly and approaches sometimes even more so. Therefore, we do have to take into account what our colleagues further up the system are looking to use the information for and work together to make sure that any recording is both useful and relevant and supports the children's ongoing learning. As a former Key Stage One teacher myself, I know

that teachers in Key Stage One are generally looking for the same things as in early years: information which clearly shows them what experiences the children have already had and where the children are with their learning so that they can take that starting point and move forward with it.

How do we record?

Having established that we are all looking at recording children's learning experiences for the same reasons, we now have to look at how we record in early years. This is largely driven by a commitment to what learning looks like within our setting. The proposed EYFS framework places huge emphasis on the provision of learning through well planned, purposeful play. This is how research has shown that children across the world learn best, it's what we are doing and it should be what we are recording.

The very nature of children's play does not lend itself to sitting down and writing everything on a piece of paper. The reason why the draft EYFS framework places communication and language as a prime area of learning separately to literacy is because much of what children do is through speech, language and other forms of communication and therefore our records should and must reflect this emphasis. Recording should show creatively the ways you have helped the children to explore learning through planned, purposeful play. It therefore stands to reason that the recording should, in theory, be as creative as the play it portrays.

Step away from the pencil!

Time and time again, I see practitioners offering children the chance to 'draw what you saw' or 'write what we did' and I have to suppress the urge to scream loudly! In these instances, the learning has already happened and the need to 'squirrel' or hoard paper just to show that a task has been completed seems both pointless for the children and unhelpful to the practitioner (unless of course your objective was to analyse the finer points of the child's handwriting skills!). In early years (and I would hope throughout school) we should be looking at the learning we are witnessing and how best we can show that learning.

This often calls for a creative solution. It stands to reason that if the learning comes in the form of a child talking and telling you what they are doing as they do it, then the recording must be of that speech. Here you have two options. One, you can hand-write annotations of what the child said (an early years practitioner should always be armed with a pad of sticky notes and a pen!) or two, you can invest in equipment to allow either you or ideally the children to record their investigation and discussion.

Most digital cameras now come with built-in video mode which offers a great way of recording learning as does a cheap digital voice recorder. There are more expensive solutions on the market ranging from hand-held video cameras for the children which are virtually indestructible, to small re-recordable cards which can be used to record children's comments (they make great additions to interactive displays as children can visit and revisit their thoughts and questions).

If you video a session or a child's comments, you can then save them to disc and include the disc within the child's written learning journal. It is about you, the practitioner being committed to the fact that an annotated photograph shows a child's learning so much better than a forced piece of writing or a chart.

I'm not saying don't do charts with young children to record findings (they are after all, a skill that can be demonstrated) but an annotated picture of a group making the chart or sorting with individual comments annotated is much more informative of a child's learning than the actual chart itself.

So when thinking about recording science exploration, investigation and learning, be knowledgeable about what learning is going on, be mindful of the many ways in which learning can show itself and be creative with the ways in which you record what you witness. Do not record for the sake of recording and definitely don't do it because someone else says they want it. Know your children, know their needs, and be proud to show all that they do in your setting.

Science through popular stories

There will be times when lots of science learning comes spontaneously out of other areas of play within your continuous provision and there will also be times when the children's interests and questions lead you into some exciting and amazing discoveries. There will, however, be other times when you have identified a joint interest or a learning need and you are looking to plan an open-ended science activity to inspire the children and focus them on a particular science skill such as asking questions or using equipment. Questioning which leads to open-ended discovery is best rooted in children's play and familiar scenarios. This chapter will look at some of the activities you could introduce to your children to set them off on such a path of discovery.

Using stories

I have chosen to use popular stories as a starting point for these 'science challenges', not only because they give children a comfortable starting point but because many adults who feel less confident in 'teaching' or leading science feel happier with the familiar focus of a story. There are, of course, hundreds of children's stories out there which could be used as a stimulus for science and I have chosen only a few, but I hope to give you some ideas and inspire you to go back through your book collection and spot the science potential within.

You will also notice that I have steered away from some traditional stories which have been used for decades as a stimulus for science-based discussion. This is not about using a story to start a discussion about a science based theme (*The Hungry Caterpillar* by Eric Carle, for example, is often used to start a discussion about caterpillars and butterflies). My approach is about 'doing science' not talking about it. It is about the story being a starting point for investigation and how, by giving the children access to lots of varied resources they can and will find the answers to your open-ended questions in their own way (not necessarily in the way you expect!).

For each of the stories I have provided suggestions for the type of resources you could collect in anticipation of a potential investigation. However, you will need to allow children access to many more resources as you can never really be sure what direction they will go in. Then, as well as offering suggestions for an open-ended question you may like to present the children with (remember they may come up with their own and these need to be recorded for future exploration) I have also tried to acknowledge ways that the exploration could impact on other areas of provision. I have provided ideas, where appropriate, of other investigations which may stem from it.

Handa's Surprise

by Eileen Browne (Walker Books)

Science challenge question: 'What's inside?'

Resources

- **a collection of exotic and seasonal fruits** (you may like to include mango, passion fruit, papaya, coconut, pineapple, lime, lemon, orange, satsuma, kiwi fruit, dragon fruit, pomegranate and banana as well as familiar fruits such as apples, pears and berries)

- **plastic knives and spoons**

- **sharp knife** (for adult use only)

NB: When working with food always make sure that you are aware of any potential food allergies and take good food hygiene precautions.

What to do

This is a well-used story in most early years settings. It is a lovely, brightly-illustrated book and tells the story of Handa and her journey to visit friends and family and share her collection of tropical fruits. This is great for getting children to explore fruits they may be unfamiliar with, and forces them to fall back on their instinct of using all of their senses to explore the fruits. Initially, just have the fruits available when you ask the science challenge question.

Only provide the knives and spoons when the children identify a need. It may be quite some time before they have exhausted their own means of opening the fruit by peeling, biting, squashing and so on and they ask for extra help.

As the children are exploring the question, encourage them to use all of their senses to explore the fruits and to talk about what they find. (Dragon fruit looks strange, smells even stranger and is an acquired taste!). The discovery of seeds inside the fruits can then lead on to other investigations about how to grow seeds and what will grow if we plant them. Finding out how to get inside a coconut can be a whole investigation in itself!

Pause for thought

Do not be tempted to lead where this exploration goes by starting to cut the fruit up. Let the children decide how they are going to rise to the science challenge.

This activity is often planned to build on children's knowledge of fruits, foods and seeds but I would argue that it can equally well be planned as an exploring the senses activity (much more fun than sniffing a few scented yoghurt pots!).

Can't You Sleep, Little Bear?

by Martin Waddell and Barbara Firth
(Walker Books)

Science challenge question: 'What can you see in the dark?'

Resources

- **large black or navy sheets**

- **selection of torches** – wind up, battery operated, solar powered, dynamo

- **lots of different light-up toys** (easily available from supermarkets and pound shops)

- **foil survival blankets**

- **battery-operated Christmas lights**

- **glow sticks** – new and used

- **glow in the dark shapes**

- **reflective clothing**

- **fluorescent papers**

- **perspex mirrors** and other shiny objects

- **batteries** – new and used (be careful of old batteries leaking and dispose of them environmentally)

What to do

Young children love exploring with torches and quite often light and dark exploration can come out of spontaneous play with the science equipment from your investigation station. However, this story gives a great, familiar focus for children and allows them to begin to explore their existing knowledge of dark and light things.

The story explores Little Bear's struggle to get to sleep and Big Bear's battle to stem the dark with a variety of different-sized lanterns. Although it would be easy to ask children 'Which things show up in the dark den?' my challenge question asks that they have first to create their own 'dark' before they even begin to explore what they can see. The range of resources available also looks to challenge some of the children's existing knowledge about light sources.

Glow-in-the-dark stars and shapes will not show up unless they have been previously exposed to a light source. Fluorescent paper will not show up in the dark without a light source and reflective clothing needs a light source before it comes into its own. Make sure you include torches with and without batteries and also with batteries which no longer work as all of these situations offer potential for ongoing exploration and investigation.

Pause for thought

This is an investigation which needs time to evolve. Leave your dark den up so children can visit and revisit it and bring new items to try out. This can go on for weeks before interest wains.

Splash!

by Sarah Garland (Frances Lincoln)

Science challenge question: 'How can you make the most bubbles?'

Resources

- **source of water –** tray or clear storage box
- **bubble bath**
- **washing-up liquid**
- **shaving foam**
- **shower gel**
- **baby shampoo**
- **big bubble mixture** (see below)
- **toothpaste**
- **whisks**
- **straws** (different lengths, sizes, shapes)
- **spoons**
- **water play syringes**
- **turkey baster**
- **plastic tubing**

Big bubble mixture

What you need:

- 1 litre water
- 70ml concentrated washing-up liquid
- 20ml glycerine (available from pharmacists)

What to do:

1. Mix together the water, washing-up liquid and glycerine gently. Try not to whip up bubbles as you mix. Leave to settle overnight and use with bubble wands as usual or try with a big hoola hoop!

2. Experiment with adding more glycerine – a bit more should help to make bigger bubbles!

What to do

This book shows that you don't have to have a complicated text to start a great science challenge. It shows that picture books can be just as much a stimulus as more complex titles.

The science challenge question allows children to explore whatever combination of resources they prefer to try and make as many bubbles as they can. The question deliberately does not ask 'What can make the most bubbles?' as this could lead to a focus on the equipment or the bubble-making mixtures. Here the children are free to choose their focus and their own variables.

This activity can then be revisited over a period of days and weeks, each time changing something slightly to allow the children the chance to explore the same thinking within a different scenario.

Variables can include changing the colour and the temperature of the water on offer; the size of the containers being used (from small individual bowls where children can explore on their own to big paddling pools in the outdoor area and everything in between). Also try changing the things they can add to the water (mud, glitter, sand and so on).

The question does not actually mention water so be prepared for some alternatives such as muddy bubbles and frothy juice!

NB: Be mindful of skin allergies when adding products to water and always ensure safe water play practices are adhered to.

Alternative texts for the same challenge include:
Honk! by Mick Inkpen (Hodder Children's Books)
Badger's Bath by Nick Butterworth (Collins)

Pause for thought

This activity highlights the importance of children revisiting and reviewing their thinking in lots of different situations. Children need to try, try again and try some more with science skills and knowledge so that they can grow, challenge and formulate their own understanding of how their discoveries relate to their world as a whole.

The Lighthouse keeper's Lunch

by Ronda and David Armitage (Scholastic)

Science challenge question: 'What could she have put in the sandwiches?'

Resources

- **bread** (white and brown)

- **plastic knives** (for spreading)

- **lots of different sandwich fillings, you may like to include:**

  - mustard
  - jam
  - marmalade
  - Marmite
  - lemon curd
  - chocolate spread (not with nuts in)
  - mint sauce
  - apple sauce
  - chocolate ice-cream sauce
  - sweet pickle
  - cake sprinkles
  - ice-cream sprinkles

What to do

This popular story tells of the poor lighthouse keeper whose lunch keeps getting eaten by seagulls on the journey from land to the lighthouse. The story follows the lighthouse keeper's wife's quest to stop the seagulls by adding various things to the basket, including a cat and some mustard sandwiches.

The idea behind this activity is to leave the sandwich-making to the children. By providing lots of different sweet and savoury ingredients for the children to explore and use you are opening up the potential and encouraging a great, fun, multi-sensory investigation. Try using supermarket own brands as there are generally very few picture clues as to the contents of packages, which then forces children to use their senses to explore the contents and decide whether to use them or not.

Alternative story: *Sam's Sandwich* by David Pelham (Jonathan Cape)

Pause for thought

Do not be tempted to let adult preconceived ideas about what things may taste like influence what the children use. You may not think chocolate spread and mint sauce sounds nice but the children may love it!

NB: As with all food-based activities be aware of any potential food allergies and take good food hygiene precautions.

Ethical factors

Some people have difficulty with the concept of children exploring food as part of their play in light of famine in other parts of the world. If this is an issue, you may choose not to offer the activity or consider donating an equal amount of money to an overseas aid project or additional food to a local food bank. Use as much of the food in these activities as part of ongoing play and snack provision and then look at a composter to dispose of waste in an environmentally-friendly way (a worm-based one is great for even more science learning!).

The Happy Hedgehog Band

by Martin Waddell and Jill Barton
(Candlewick Press)

Science challenge question: 'Can you make a sound?'

Resources

- **variety of containers in different sizes, shapes and materials.** Include plastic pots and plates, metal saucepans and bowls and wooden utensils

- **lots of items to be used as beaters** (spoons in different materials: wooden, metal, plastic)

- **string**

- **elastic bands**

- **rulers**

- **access to premade instruments**

- **pots and junk-modelling materials**

- **metal jingle bells** (be aware of choking hazards with certain sizes)

- **open access to outdoors and your creative area**

What to do

This lovely story sees a happy group of hedgehog friends form a band and perform their catchy tune. They are eventually joined by lots of other forest animals making their own sounds. It is a great stimulus for thinking about noises and sounds, as well as a chance to explore the sound-making potential of different materials. The open-endedness of the science challenge question leaves children free to make whatever noise they want indoors or outdoors. By providing lots of different materials the children have the opportunity to bang, shake, rub and blow things and to explore sound freely without being channelled by the adults.

Pause for thought

Don't be tempted to make the selection of resources available too narrow as this will restrict any choices the children make. You may think it might be nice to make a musical shaker but the children may prefer to follow the drum theme of the book. We have to be ever aware of how limiting access to resources can limit choices and learning potential and also how our own perception of what might be interesting is not necessarily what a child thinks is interesting. (And you have to ask yourself exactly what science is being learnt by sitting in a group and all making shakers.)

More story suggestions

There are many, many ways that stories can be used as a starting point for open-ended questioning and subsequent science exploration and discovery. As children become more used to being able to follow their own route of enquiry from story-based questioning they are more likely to ask questions from other stories. I could write a whole book just on the science challenge questions from children's books. Here are just a few more suggestions that you may like to try. Make sure you use a good spread of contemporary and traditional stories.

Title	Science challenge question	Science learning potential
The Three Little Pigs	Can you build a house? Can you blow a house down?	The open-ended question gives children the chance to build their house from whatever they like, indoors or outdoors. Provide access to lots of building and modelling materials, as well as construction kits and cardboard boxes (big and small). Let the children explore where they want with what they want.
The Blue Balloon by Mick Inkpen (Hodder Children's Books)	What's inside a balloon?	Let the children have free reign to add things to their balloon (rice, sand, flour, glitter, tissue paper etc) as well as providing balloon pumps so they can fill them with air as well if they like. This activity allows children to explore materials and to develop their own personal solutions to a single question. NB: Always practise good balloon safety – broken pieces of balloon can be a choking hazard and should be disposed of immediately.
The Three Billy Goats Gruff	Can you build a bridge?	Again, like The Three Little Pigs, this gives children open access to explore both indoors and outdoors. Building bridges with blocks, planks, crates, boxes, play dough or construction bricks all helps children to explore what things are made of and the forces that help them to stack and/or fall.
What's in The Witch's Kitchen? by Nick Sharratt (Walker Books)	Can you make soup?	As well as having a wide variety of fruit and vegetables available for children to access and explore, let them have free choice on what they add to their soup. They may decide to make it in the role-play house, outdoors in the digging area with mud or just on a huge scale by adding vegetables to the water tray! This is a great way to explore the material properties of lots of vegetables as well as building on their understanding of water or sand.
Goldilocks and The Three Bears	Can you make porridge?	This is a great one for offering as part of messy play. Let the children choose from a wide variety of ingredients (including porridge oats, instant porridge, powdered mash potato, jelly crystals, food colourings and essences, water, milk, bubble mixture, glitter etc) and let them mix away! Offer oversized wooden spoons (you can get them up to one metre long!) for mixing for extra excitement. This allows children to explore materials in a really exciting way with lots of fun and mess! Alternatively use The Magic Porridge Pot story.

Title	Science challenge question	Science learning potential
Mrs Mopple's Washing Line by Anita Hewitt and Robert Broomfield (Red Fox)	Can you wash the clothes? Can you dry the clothes?	This activity allows children to explore water and different soap (bubble-making) materials with a purpose. It can take lots of different directions, from exploring the amount or size of the bubbles in the water, to which clean the clothes best and how the clothes can be dried. Remember to let the children guide which direction the exploration takes. Alternative text: *Wash Day!* by Sue Baker and Jess Stockham (Child's Play).
Peace At Last by Jill Murphy (Macmillan Children's Books)	What can you hear?	This activity encourages children to find ways of listening and recording their findings both indoors and outdoors. Den-making outdoors is a great way of making a space for listening. The activity lends itself to letting children explore ICT equipment such as video recorders, cameras and voice recorders as a creative means of capturing the sounds. (It doesn't always have to be about putting pencil to paper!)
We're Going On a Bear Hunt by Michael Rosen and Helen Oxenbury (Walker Books)	Can you go on a bear hunt?	This question encourages children to explore indoors and out using all of their senses in the hunt for the ever-illusive bear. Don't forget to include the chance to make a noise by splashing through the water or squelching through the mud. Follow-on activities can include 'We're going on a smell hunt' (much more fun than sniffing those yoghurt pots!) or 'We're going on a sound hunt', the scope is endless.
Jasper's Beanstalk by Nick Butterworth and Mick Inkpen (Hodder Children's Books)	Can you grow a bean?	Allow children access to whatever materials they want (sand, mud, flour, cornflour etc) to be able to plant their bean. Have areas where they can plant and dig up beans (like Jasper) and areas where beans can be left to grow. This is a great way to explore the child-led approach to a very traditionally adult-led activity. Alternative text: *Ten Seeds* by Ruth Brown (Knopf Books).

Science in partnership with parents

There are two things in education that we are often guilty of losing sight of:

1 Parents are the experts on their own children.

2 Children continue to learn even when they are not within our settings.

As science learning is very much about the children making sense of their world (both inside and outside of our settings), it is vital that we look at the contribution that positive partnerships with parents can make to a child's overall learning potential. There are many things you can do to get parents actively involved in early science learning.

All early years frameworks across the UK place massive emphasis on the benefits of working together with parents for the benefit of children's well-being and development. My personal commitment to working in partnership with parents stems not only from my years in settings where I have witnessed firsthand the benefits of working closely with parents, but also because I am a mother of a five year old. I am passionate about knowing what the practitioners are doing with my precious offspring and what learning they are having the privilege of seeing (and which I am sadly missing)!

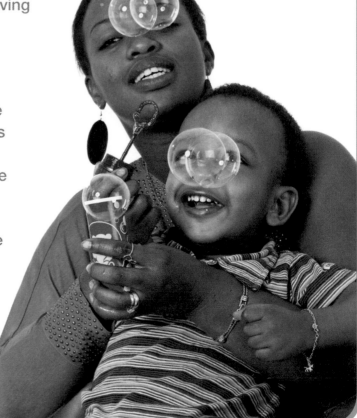

The key to good working partnerships with parents is communication. We, the practitioners, have to find creative ways of communicating what we do with the children and why. Wherever possible we should encourage parents to become a part of this learning process. I can't offer a comprehensive solution to these issues (that's a whole other book!) but what I can do is suggest some small things that you can do to build up these relationships and hopefully enhance children's scientific learning as well as their thirst for exploration and discovery.

Communicating what we have done and why

There are a great deal of mechanisms that are probably already in place in your setting for communicating what you have done with children on a daily basis and the kinds of learning experiences they may have encountered. These might include: daily information sheets, books or slips and open access to children's learning journals or profiles (although do not assume that parents automatically know that they are allowed to look at these whenever they want or in fact where to find them).

However, there is always more that we can do to improve on this communication. We have to continuously review our settings from a parents' perspective and, in doing so, we may realise that the amount of learning that parents actually see/hear about is limited (as any parent who has uttered those immortal words 'What did you do today?' will tell you!).

So what can we be doing to build on the levels of information our parents have about the kinds of learning their children are being given access to?

Displaying learning processes

It's worth looking around your setting and asking yourself whether the displays on your walls reflect your learning processes or just the products of these processes? If the walls are adorned with posters, colourful paintings and collages then you may like to look at different ways of displaying learning processes in your settings.

Much science learning comes in the form of talk and exploration as part of the children's ongoing play. It is this discussion and exploration that should be the focus for your science displays. Learn to use lots of photographs annotated with speech bubbles and interspersed with descriptions of what the children did, said or thought. In this way not only do children have a focus for revisiting their investigations and explorations but parents can gain a wonderful insight into the kinds of learning that comes out of playing in the water tray or building a den to watch the bird table.

Policies and practices

Not all parents get the chance to come into the setting on a regular basis. A childminder or grandparent may be the main point of contact and we need to look at ways of conveying what we do and why to all parents, even those we rarely get to see. (Do not assume that just because you do not see them, the parents are not committed and involved in helping their children to continue to develop outside of the setting.)

There are some lovely parent information leaflets available which explain in no-nonsense language the purpose of various different areas of early learning (see **www.early-education.org.uk**) but you may like to look at putting together your own series of information leaflets which can be sent out to parents. Look at explaining (briefly) what your policies and practice are, what this will look like to the children (what they will be doing in your setting) and the kinds of learning which can come from these activities. As well as focusing parents' thinking on a specific area of learning which they might be able to help their child with, it also goes some way to getting over the 'all they do is play' obstacle that many practitioners think they face.

Make sure that, as well as sending out copies of your leaflets, you have some available in communal areas that parents can access and additional copies they can take home with them. Be mindful of children whose parents may be separated and offer additional copies so both parents are able to help where they can. Parents who lead busy working lives may find an emailed version easier to access alongside a downloadable online bank of documents on your website.

Painting outdoors

Messy play week!

Focus weeks

Some settings have developed focus weeks where they concentrate on a particular area of learning through play with the aim of heightening parents' awareness of what they do and how this benefits their children. I recently witnessed a 'Messy play week' at a pre-school where, as well as sending out leaflets about the benefits of messy play (including recipes for parents to try at home), the parents were able to come into the setting and join in with the messy play activities and learn alongside their children. One parent commented to me, 'The washing machine was on constantly that week, but she had a great time and I can see how much she gets out of it now!'

When having a focus week, make sure you have a display of learning somewhere where parents can see it (in the entrance hall or on an outside window facing where parents wait is ideal) to highlight what you have done and why you are doing it.

Annotated photos

As part of displaying your learning processes, and for your learning journals, you will be printing photographs of the children learning and annotating them. Also annotate the back of any display photos so you can then pass them on to the parents as you refresh and change the display, offering them a precious glimpse of their child's learning. If you want to take this further, you could look at ways of securely emailing parents a picture of their child during the day with a 'Look what I'm doing mummy!' comment or provide secure access to a daily gallery on your website.

Working together to explore science

As well as providing a much wider range of information to parents about what we do and why we do it, there is much we can do to build on actually working together with parents to help the children grow and learn.

Workshops, open days and fun days

Try offering workshops to parents in evenings or on Saturday mornings, where they can come and take part in science-based activities (like those included in this book) and enjoy learning together. This will give you a chance to get the message across about what you do to enhance learning in your setting and what the children gain from this.

Then try organizing an open day where there is a heavy science focus for activities and where parents can join in alongside their children.

If you get really enthusiastic, you could then try a science fun day where lots of science-based activities are open to parents, carers, siblings and the wider community.

Science shared challenge board

On a smaller scale, it is nice to offer a shared science challenge either regularly or occasionally where all parents are challenged to answer a question with their children at home and are then encouraged to bring in evidence of their findings in the form of photos, videos, collection bags and so on. Display these prominently to show that you value learning in partnership in your setting.

Shared science challenges could include:

- 'How high can you bounce a ball?'

- 'What's the biggest bubble you can make?'

- 'How many different-coloured objects can you find on your way home?'

- 'What sounds can you hear on the way to nursery/school?'

Encouraging science at home

As well as building up a bank of ideas for shared science challenges, it is worth developing a bank of science-based activity ideas that children can do at home with their parents which are both fun, exciting and which build on things you are already doing in your setting. Why not try offering a sheet about how to make a balloon hovercraft or watching racing raisins (see page 61). Many of the activities suggested within this book can be easily adapted for use at home as they stem primarily from children's play-based exploration.

Home environments sometimes offer situations to explore and enhance thinking which has been started in the setting, but in a unique way. Suggestions for bathtime explorations or kitchen cupboard science activities are great for getting parents playing and exploring with their children at the same time as learning science! If parents get really enthusiastic about home-based science, then make available copies of science activity books with extra ideas for them to try. You may like to develop sheets for some of the following ideas:

Bathtime science activities:

- Shaving foam painting – mix shaving foam with a little food colouring (not too much or you may stain the bath or the children!) and allow children to paint with it on the side of the bath. It helps children to explore textures, materials and colour mixing as well as developing their understanding about floating and sinking as the mixture will float in the bath.

- Sinking super heroes – in settings children have the chance to explore water play in trays, tubs and containers. At home they get a unique opportunity to explore water play while being 'in' the water while in the bath or shower. Encourage children to play with character figures and plastic animals (make sure they don't contain batteries) in the bath. Exploring superheroes diving or toy sharks floating, helps to build on their understanding while they have lots of storytelling fun.

- Whisking up a storm – at home, encourage children to have a wide range of equipment in their bathtime play. Include items for pouring in different shapes and sizes, items for whisking up bubbles (spoons and whisks) as well as funnels, sieves and turkey basters.

- Bubbling baths – allow children to explore potion and mixture-making at bathtime by adding a little food colouring to the water and letting them mix it with some bicarbonate of soda. It is harmless and forms the basis of most commercially-available fizzing bath bombs and is used in baking to make your cakes rise!

Kitchen science activities:

- Puffy painting – mix paints up using the following recipe:

  What you need:

  - 1 tablespoon self-raising flour
  - 1 tablespoon salt
  - Water and food colouring or poster paint to colour

  What to do:

  ① Mix up until you have a nice thick paste. Paint on to thick card.

  ② Adult to microwave the painting in ten second blasts until the paint has puffed up and is nice and dry. (Usually takes about 30 seconds.)

  NB: Never let children touch microwaved items until they have cooled sufficiently.

- Changing states – ice and Mentos mints will make lemonade fizz and froth up; salt will make ice melt and refreeze while cornflour and water makes a thick gloopy substance that behaves like both a solid and a liquid at the same time (see page 29). Bicarbonate of soda added to vinegar or lemon juice will produce a great frothing fizzing mixture.

- Salt crystals – fill a glass jar three-quarters full with water. Add in salt and stir until it has all dissolved. Keep adding more salt until no more will dissolve. Tie a short piece of string or cotton (about half the depth of the jar) on to a pencil and place the pencil across the neck of the jar allowing the string to dangle in the salt solution. Leave the jar in a warmish place such as a kitchen window and watch over a few days. Salt crystals will begin to grow on the string as the water in the salt solution begins to evaporate leaving the salt behind. Add a bit of food colouring to the solution and see if you can grow coloured crystals.

- Potion commotion – allow children to experiment with mixing their own potions and mixtures. Offer a range of coloured liquids (water, white vinegar, lemonade and lemon juice can all be coloured with food colouring) as well as cornflour, bicarbonate of soda and ice cubes.

Also see: Frothy volcanoes (page 62) and Cola fountains (page 63).

Other science activities:

- Ice sculptures – place collections of items into foil ice trays and freeze to make hanging ice sculptures (see page 40).

- Miniature nature collections – give children small empty matchboxes and challenge them to see how many things they can find in their garden or on a walk to the woods or a park that will fit inside the matchbox.

- Trip strips – take a piece of card (about 3cm x 20cm) and stick on a piece of double sided tape (leave one side covered). At the park or on a walk, take the remaining strip off to reveal the sticky tape and ask children to stick on things they find on their walk. It's much easier than trying to retrieve things from pockets upon your return and is a great visual aid for displays and discussion upon your return.

Science through stories at home

Many early years settings now have a collection of story sacks or bags which they lend to parents to encourage discussion and activities based around popular stories. Some have even expanded this idea to make maths story sacks with a focus on numeracy activities and games. Why not try making some science story bags or boxes based around popular stories? Use some of the ideas from stories in the previous chapter as a starting point. Look for opportunities to encourage science exploration through messy play, water and sand play and outdoor learning at home. Include books, simple equipment such as a pair of binoculars or a magnifier and some activity suggestions.

Examples of science story bag:

- *The Very Hungry Caterpillar* – a magnifying glass and a bug hunt picture chart.

- *We're Going on a Bear Hunt* – a pair of binoculars.

Out and about information

Parents are often unaware of the rich variety of attractions and places to visit that can be accessed locally (often very cheaply). Many supermarkets now have stands with free leaflets about local attractions which you can collect and display in your setting. Include good places to visit that promote science thinking in the wider world. Farms, parks and woodlands are all great. Local play associations lay on cheap (often free) activities throughout the year as do local woodland trusts and park authorities. Many will offer family bug hunts or woodland craft sessions. Contact your local council or tourist information centre for details and help to offer parents more opportunities to explore the world with their children.

Science at home activity ideas

Balloon hovercraft

This is a great way of recycling some of your old plastic drinks bottles and scratched CDs.

You will need:

- an old CD

- plastic bottle top with pull-up spout

- glue and sticky tape

- balloon

- balloon pump

What to do:

1. Clean and dry your bottle top, your CD and a smooth table or floor surface.

2. Glue the cap of the bottle over the hole in the centre of the CD so that there are no gaps around the outside (an extra piece of tape helps to ensure this).

3. Press down the spout on the bottle cap so that it is fully closed.

4. Blow up your balloon and twist the neck, allowing you to put the balloon on to the bottle top spout without losing all of your air.

5. Untwist the balloon neck so that it stands up on top of the hovercraft.

6. When you are ready, carefully pull up the spout allowing the air to flow through and under the CD. Gently push your CD and see it sail across the table or the floor. How far can you get yours to go before the air runs out? Can you race each other with your hovercrafts?

Racing raisins

This idea is brilliant for keeping children amused for hours!

You will need:

- a large bottle of fizzy drink (fizzy water or cheap lemonade are fine)

- a handful of dried raisins or currants (the drier and wrinklier the better)

What to do:

1. Remove the label from the bottle so you can see inside easily.

2. Take off the lid of the bottle and add some raisins. Put the top back on as quickly as you can.

3. Watch as the raisins, initially sink, then float to the top before sinking again. This goes on and on for ages.

4. To revive the raisins, just release some of the gas from the bottle by undoing the top and doing it up again. The raisins will start bobbing again!

What is happening?

As the raisins sink through the liquid, they pick up some of the gas which is escaping from the drink. The bumpier the raisins, the more surface there is for the bubbles to stick to. As the raisin collects more and more bubbles, it eventually becomes light enough to float to the top where the bubble bursts, allowing the raisin to sink down once more.

Cola fountain

You will need:

- 1 large bottle of diet cola (2 litres)

- 1 packet of mints (Mentos are best)

- 2 pieces of card or 1 piece and a length of plastic tube wide enough to sit the mints in on top of each other

- sticky tape

What to do:

1. Put the bottle on to the ground outside and take the cap off carefully. (This has the potential to go about four metres in the air so make sure it is a long way from anything precious.)

2. Roll one piece of card into a tube wide enough to fit the neck of the bottle and tape it in place.

3. Unwrap the mints and place them into the paper tube.

4. Place the second piece of card under the end of the tube and stand it on top of the neck of the bottle.

5. When you are ready pull the bottom card out allowing the mints to fall into the cola.

6. Get out of the way - FAST!

To ensure a bigger and better fountain:

- Use diet cola, as the sweetners in it react better with the mints.

- Sit the bottle in the sun for a while before this experiment to warm the cola.

- Make a geyser tube by sticking a metal washer over one end of a length of plastic tube. Using this instead of the paper tube forces the frothing cola mixture up through a smaller hole and the mixture under pressure will go higher.

Why does it work?

The fizzy drink contains carbon dioxide gas which has been forced into it under pressure. Undoing the lid of the bottle releases some of the pressure and allows some of the gas to appear as bubbles. Adding mints (which under a microscope look like golf balls with bumpy surfaces) gives more surface for the bubbles to stick to. With more bubbles rising to the surface they soon want to escape and do so quickly up through the neck of the bottle taking the cola with them.

Frothy volacnoes

You will need:

- a tray – cat litter tray (unused) or big turkey roasting tin are ideal

- play sand

- yoghurt pot

- white vinegar

- red food colouring

- bicarbonate of soda

What to do:

1. Place the yoghurt pot on to the tray and build the sand up around it until you have a volcano shape with the yoghurt pot as the crater at the top.

2. Add a couple of tablespoons of bicarbonate of soda to the yogurt pot.

3. Separately make up a mixture of white vinegar and red food colouring (lemon juice can be used instead of vinegar or combined with it for extra effect!).

4. Using a plastic water play syringe or a turkey baster, add some of the red liquid to the top of your volcano and watch as it froths red lava up over the top and down the sides. Add more liquid to keep the reaction going.

Summary

Hopefully you can now see that science in early years is truly imbedded in almost all early years play experiences. The ability to be inquisitive and curious and to have the confidence to explore and investigate the world is key to life-long learning skills. It is far from being a scary, untouchable subject full of jargon and impossible ideas but is about us as humans working together to make sense of this wonderful and ever changing world around us. I hope this book has given you some ideas to help you to begin to make emerging science skills central to your planning and provision and to begin to put the 'wow' factor back into science for both you and the children you work with.

Bibliography

De Boo, M. (1999) Science 3-6: *Laying the Foundations in the Early Years Association for Science Education*, London.

DfE (2011) *Statutory Framework for The Early Years Foundation Stage* – Draft for Consultation

DfE, London

DFES (2007) *The Early Years Foundation Stage: Setting the Standards for Learning, Development and Care for Children from birth to five* DFES, London

Harriman, H. (2006) *The Outdoor Classroom – A Place to Learn* A Corner to Learn Ltd, Swindon

Leicestershire Early Years Team, *Outdoor Learning: www.leics.gov.uk/outdoor_learning_publication-2.pdf*

Ruddock, G. et al (2004) *Where England Stands in the Trends in International Mathematics and Science Study* cited in Oliver, A (2006) Creative Teaching Science in the Early Years & Primary Classroom David Fulton Publishers, London

Singer, D. and Revenson, T. (1996): *A Piaget Primer: How a Child Thinks* Penguin Books USA Inc, New York